AVIA᷄

AERONAU

INNS ᴏғ ʙʀɪᴛᴀɪɴ

C000241566

Dave Smith with Ken Ellis

Midland Publishing Limited

Dedicated to all of those people past, present and future who undertake arduous research into this subject!

Copyright © 1996 Dave Smith and Ken Ellis
ISBN 1 85780 048 6

Published by
Midland Publishing Limited
24 The Hollow, Earl Shilton
Leicester, LE9 7NA, England

Design concept and layout
© Midland Publishing Limited and Stephen Thompson Associates

Printed in England by
Woolnough Bookbinding Limited
Irthlingborough, Northamptonshire

Title Page Illustration:
'The Wheatsheaf' at Upper Benefield, Northants, 'watering hole' for the 401st Bomb Group, Deenethorpe. Ken Ellis

CONTENTS

INTRODUCTION

Pub names and their origins are a fascinating study in their own right, with many taking their titles from aspects of history local, national and international. In its relatively brief life, aviation has been a fruitful source of inspiration from early birdmen and balloons, to Concorde and space flight.

The Romans are generally credited with introducing inn signs to Britain. In later years, the gatehouses and lodges of the nobility offered refreshment to weary travellers and signs displayed the coat of arms of the lord of the manor. Hence such names as 'The Red Lion' and 'The Rose and Crown'.

Unfortunately, today's pub names rarely offer any guarantee of permanency in their commemoration of history, aviation or otherwise. They are subject to the whims of the brewery chains, individual landlords, and fluctuating fashions but happily, some have kept their names for many years, supported by tradition and local opinion.

This book is not claimed to be exhaustive and some of the names have already become history. It is aimed to be the first major step in tackling an interesting and frequently amusing subject. The authors have relied heavily on the experiences and observations of friends and look forward to contributions from readers so that the second edition can benefit from a wider set of 'eyes' (and throats!). Letters and photographs will be welcomed at: 24, The Hollow, Earl Shilton, Leicester, LE9 7NA.

This ever-changing vista does give the student of aeronautical pubs and inns limitless scope to keep going back and checking up on previously discovered delights and provides a great excuse for initiating a relentless search for new ones!

Dave Smith
Ken Ellis
June 1996

Acknowledgements

Alan Allen, Dave Allport of *AIR International* (but for the purposes of this work seconded to sister journal *FlyPast!*), Tim Crowe, Fred Cubberley, Alan Curry, Peter Green, Annette Harrison and Bob Payne, Graham Buchan Innes, Mike Ingham, Alan and Shirley Mildred, Rod Priddle, Paul Shaw, Tom Singfield, Peter Spooner, Bill Taylor, David E Thompson.

John Denton for the cartoons.

Chris Salter and Steve Thompson at Midland Publishing

And of course to all the publicans, landlords and landladies who have helped in their own special ways!

NOTES

The study of pub names has long been established and there are several ways of expanding such a hobby – see 'You Want More?'. Studying the 'sub-culture' of aeronautical pubs and inns has to date been a much more fragmented business.

The amateur aviation press – often a rich source of pioneering notions – has largely left this subject alone. The first professional journal to touch on the subject was, surprisingly, *Flight*, with two light-hearted pieces in August and December 1961. It then fell to Leslie Hunt to write on the subject in the magazine *High Road* of February 1970. An enlarged version of this then appeared in the *RAF Souvenir Book* for 1971. After that *Air Pictorial* and *Aviation News* featured the subject once in a while and since 1981 *FlyPast* dipped into the subject on an occasional basis.

Both authors have long been fascinated with aviation pubs and inns. Dave Smith has written extensively on the subject, with some material also appearing in his book *Britain's Aviation Memorials and Mementoes* (Patrick Stephens, Sparkford 1992) and a major article appeared in the now-defunct *Aviation News* in December 1993. Dave and Ken Ellis collaborated in a full colour booklet *An Introduction to Aeronautical Pubs and Inns in Britain* presented free with the October 1994 issue of *FlyPast*.

Both authors have long believed that there was scope for a wider and deeper study, the result you now see before you.

The section 'What's in a Name?' deals with what most people would consider to be the full scope of the subject – pubs and inns with aeronautical names or connections. 'Watering Holes' is but a fleeting attempt to look at the 'flavour' of pubs that were frequented by wartime flyers. Some pay tribute to their former 'trade', others are oblivious to the connections they may have had with wartime Britain. There is an inevitable overlap bet-ween 'What's in a Name?' and 'Watering Holes'.

At no point are the authors attempting to recommend any establishment in any terms, eg beer, food, service etc. That is a judgement that readers must make for themselves!

'Planes and Pints' claims only to be an introduction to the concept of aircraft located at, or even within, the pub restaurant or nightclub in question. This arises partially from the increase in the number of airframes that are known to have been installed in 'nite spots' across Britain.

'You Want More?' tries to show how more information can be gleaned and how readers may wish to go out and find new venues of their own.

The 'Gazetteer' attempts to index the names mentioned and to give greater details of those pubs and inns believed to be current.

WHAT'S IN A NAME?

Pubs and Inns
with aeronautical names
and connections

PIONEERING DAYS

The dawn of flight has left us with many names connected with ballooning, 'The Air Balloon' being a popular one. The best known is on Birdlip Hill, overlooking Gloucester. The site was popular with early balloonists from 1784. The 'Air Balloons' main road position makes it one of Britain's best-known aeronautical pubs. The interior is very pleasant with plenty of 'balloonalia' to catch the eye. The pub sign has changed. In 1977 it featured a gas balloon with a Union Jack design on the envelope, with a somewhat tenuous-looking basket that included what the early aeronauts called 'influencers' to try and steer the contraption. The current sign shows two gas balloons over the Cotswolds, one of which appears to be decidedly in trouble!

Not far away is the 'Air Balloon Tavern' in Air Balloon Road, St George's, in Bristol, a substantial urban pub. Its pub sign has an intrepid hare making a flight in a gas balloon – any significance? There is another 'Air Balloon' at Abingdon Oxfordshire, and 'Balloons' at Bedford, Beds, and Newcastle-on-Tyne. The 'Balloon Inn' at Fulham carried no sign, it and the 'Balloon Tavern' at Ulcombe, Kent, are either renamed or no more.

At Lutterworth, Leicestershire, which has two more aeronautical pubs, is 'The Balloon'. 'The Gondola' at Wollaton, Nottinghamshire, refers to a hot air balloon

Below: *Birdlip's 'The Air Balloon'.* Rod Priddle   Right: *The present-day pub sign.* Ken Ellis

'The Air Balloon', Birdlip, pub sign of 1977.
Bill Taylor

'The Air Balloon Tavern', St George's,
Bristol. Rod Priddle

not a Venetian boat. A cottage nearby is named 'Balloon Cottage'.

East Yorkshire is not, perhaps, the first place that one would expect to find a pub honouring the brilliant aircraft designer Barnes Wallis. The airship base at Howden, north of Goole, became the home of The Airship Guarantee Company in 1924 and it was here that the highly successful R-100 passenger airship was built, with Wallis on the design staff. He went on to design the Wellington for Vickers, the 'bouncing bomb' and pioneer the 'swing-wing' aerodynamic concept, among many other achievements.

'The Flying Monk' at Malmesbury, Wiltshire, has sadly made way for a supermarket. It commemorated a monk's 11th century attempt to fly on makeshift wings from the abbey tower. He was lucky to escape with broken legs – the abbot banned any further attempts; the first recorded example of an anti-airport lobby! More recent pioneers were remembered by 'The Cayley Arms' at Brompton, North Yorkshire (Sir George Cayley, was a local squire and is acknowledged as the father of British aviation) and the 'Aerial Hotel' on the A4 at Heathrow. The 'Aerial' (now known as the 'Forte Poste House Aerial', has the distinction of being the first circular hotel in Europe. When opened in the late 1950s, its decor and name were taken from the inspiration of William Samuel Henson, who pioneered flight concepts with the awesome Aerial Steam Carriage of 1842. Alas, today the interior decor is of another age...

'Cody's Tree' at Farnborough, Hampshire, was named after the tree to which he tethered his aeroplane for engine runs. In the early 1980s the sign featured the much-abused tree, with a portrait of Colonel Samuel Franklin Cody in flying helmet along with images of one of his man-lifting observation kites and his Wright-like Biplane of 1908. The Biplane

made its first flight from Laffan's Plain, Farnborough, on 16th October 1908. A metal facsimile of the tree marks the spot, while sections of the gnarled trunk are preserved elsewhere for posterity.

A Wright Flyer biplane – of the sort that made the first-ever powered flight from Kill Devil Hills, Kitty Hawk, North Carolina, on 17th December 1903 – adorns the pub sign of 'The Heald Green', near Cheadle Hulme in south Manchester. To its immediate west is Manchester Airport and the choice of the Orville and Wilbur Wright's Flyer shows an appreciation of cause and effect!

On the A417 running into Gloucester at Brockworth is 'The Flying Machine'. This

The pub sign of the 'Codys [sic] Tree' as it appeared in 1981. W S Gooch via Peter Green

'The Flying Machine' remembers the Gloster factory at Hucclecote. Ken Ellis

The Wright Flyer of 1903. 'The Heald Green' near Manchester Airport features the Flyer on its pub sign. Northwest Airlines

conjures images of early aviation but the pub sign (on one side) is somewhat faded Gloster Gladiator I K7985, in the colours of 73 Squadron. This commemorates the production of such biplanes and many other illustrious types at the nearby Hucclecote factory. K7985 was indeed built at Hucclecote and entered service in 1937 with 73 Squadron, so full marks for the pub sign research. What has become the A417 was a major coaching route, and the other side of the pub sign notes this, 'The Flying Machine' also being a famous stage coach. 'The Flying Machine' at Biggin Hill is very much in the aviation mode!

The gliding site at Dunstable Downs in Bedfordshire gave us 'The Glider' and 'The Windsock'. Not far away at Henlow, Bedfordshire, 'The Parachute' followed another theme. In Chelmsford, Essex, is 'The Red Beret'. The pub sign shows a paratrooper descending, with slight artis-tic licence as he would not be wearing his famous beret at the time! The surrounding roads are all named after battles and the pub is in Arnhem Road.

The 'Airman' at Meppershall, also near Henlow, shares the name with another at Feltham, Greater London. The latter originally had a pub sign that incorporated a Gloster Gladiator. In 1971 a new pub sign was unveiled by Squadron Leader Bill Loverseed of the RAF's 'Red Arrows' formation display team. Six other members of the team were there to help out. The new sign showed a 'Red Arrow' pilot, complete with white 'bone dome' emblazoned with a red arrow. (Air Force wags joked during the currency of this 'bone dome' that the arrow was to remind pilots which way round it went on!) Behind the pilot, seven red jets, superficially the Folland Gnat T.1s that the team flew in those days, are smoking up the sky.

FIRST WORLD WAR

'The Leefe Robinson' at Harrow Weald, Greater London, lies beneath the scene of a successful and famous combat with a German airship on the night of 2nd/3rd August 1916. Royal Flying Corps pilot Lt William Leefe Robinson took off to intercept the German airship *Schütte-Lanz* SL.11 from Sutton's Farm, near Hornchurch, in a BE.2c of 39 Squadron. Tracking the SL.11 took some considerable time and distance, but eventually the giant airship was brought down, crashing near Cuffley, Hertfordshire, about 2am. Leefe Robinson was awarded the Victoria Cross for this feat on 5th September 1917.

'The Dun Horse' on the Ramsey Road, heading north out of St Ives, in Huntingdonshire (as was) changed its name in 1988 to 'The Aviator' in honour of Lt Kenneth Wastell who was killed on 29th March 1918 when his Harland & Wolff-built de Havilland DH.6 C5453 hit the spire of All Saints Church, which is next door to the pub. Wastell was thrown clear in the crash, but fell through the roof and was found, dying, among the pews. The spire of the church was also badly damaged and took a considerable time to repair.

Wastell was lost and looking for Wyton airfield, to the north west of St Ives. Heading towards St Ives from the south, he saw the expansive Great Meadows in front of the town and landed to ask directions. He took off, heading north, crossed the River Great Ouse and collided with the spire. It is possible that in the climb, with his forward view obscured, and with him probably straining to see what was to his left, ie in the direction of Wyton, Wastell was distracted.

The pub sign shows a happier scene with an aviator in a DH.6 'buzzing' the pub (which is depicted underneath the port upper wing) with All Saints Church in the background. Details of the incident can be found inside the pub.

The pub sign at 'The Aviator', showing the hapless DH.6 'buzzing' All Saints Church – a fanciful interpretation of the real incident. Bottom right, the pub itself can be seen.
Bill Taylor

Contrasts at the 'Bader Arms', Tangmere. All Ken Ellis

SECOND WORLD WAR

A famous fighter pilot who has lent his name to several pubs is Sir Douglas Bader. When Sir Douglas opened the 'Bader Arms' at Tangmere, West Sussex, he was not impressed with the awful portrait on the sign which purported to look like him. At his insistence it was redone and an acceptable likeness looks towards Tangmere aerodrome, with which he was once so closely associated. Within the busy and modern pub can be found many framed photographs, some of which do indeed reflect the life and times of Tangmere, but others seem to have been from a 'job lot'.

Today, there are two interpretations of the great pilot on the two inn signs for good measure! In mid-1995 both were looking a little worse for wear, but one carries a young Bader in blue flying overalls and scarf. On the reverse is a good painting of a Hurricane in 242 Squadron codes as 'LE-D'. The other painting of Bader shows him in later times, in suit and tie. On the other side of this is a Spitfire V with the personalised codes 'D-B' (a Spitfire bearing these marks appears on the inn sign at Portreath, Cornwall).

There is also the 'Sir Douglas Bader' at Martlesham Heath, Suffolk, opened by Bader in 1979. He also opened the 'Fighter Pilot' at Poole, Dorset, in 1970. The 'Lands End' at Woodley, Berkshire, was named so, allegedly after Bader's famous

'prang' in the Bristol Bulldog. The pub has been renamed, or is no more.

'The Cunningham' in New Addington, Surrey, named after John 'Cat's Eyes' Cunningham the night fighter ace and test pilot, seems to have been renamed. Less specific are 'The Battle of Britain' at Northfleet, and also at Kingswood, Maidstone and Dover, all in Kent. The Northfleet example, depicted a 'Dornier' going down in flames to a triumphant Spitfire. There is also a 'Battle of Britain' at Penn, near Wolverhampton, in the West Midlands, although that can hardly be regarded as 'classic' territory for 'The Few'.

Still on the fighter pilot theme, the sign for 'The Startled Saint' at West Malling, Kent, showed St Leonard looking surprised as fighter aircraft buzzed around his halo. He is a local tradition and the name imagined his reaction to the aeroplanes from the famous fighter station. Alas the pub became a private house in 1992 and the airfield has also passed into history.

A valiant local family and a Spitfire funded in their memory are commemorated by 'The Shepley Spitfire' at Totley, Sheffield, South Yorkshire. The Shepley family lived in Woodthorpe Hall, just south of Totley. The ravages of war took three of Jack Shepley's offspring, two while serving in the RAF and his daughter, who perished on the torpedoed SS *Yorkshire*.

In 1979 the new pub in Totley was named after the Spitfire Fund the area

Three Gladiators of the Fighter Flight at Hal Far, Malta, 1940. Hope *is remembered by a pub in Darlington, Durham.* Jim Pickering

organised in their memory and it was opened by Seymour, the surviving brother. (More on the Shepleys and their Spitfire on page 67.)

On the Thirsk Road, in Darlington, Durham, 'The Hope' inn sign carries an imaginative depiction of the three Gloster Sea Gladiator Is, *Faith*, *Hope* and *Charity*, which were Malta's sole air defence in the early days of the war. The aircraft, initially on charge with a unit known only as the Fighter Flight, flew their sorties largely

'The Bell' at Halton Holegate. Mike Ingham

from Hal Far on Malta against Italian SM.79 bombers and their fighter escorts to great effect from April 1940. The unit became 261 Squadron on 1st August 1940, giving up its Gladiators finally in September 1941.

The attractive sign of 'The Bell' at Halton Holegate near the wartime RAF Spilsby in Lincolnshire shows a Lancaster over the pub. Inside are a number of photographs of 44 and 207 Squadron personnel. No 44 flew Lancasters from Spilsby from September 1944 to July 1945 and 207 from October 1943 to October 1945.

'The Wild Life' at Skellingthorpe, near Lincoln, has a plaque on the wall noting that it was built just inside the main entrance of what was RAF Skellingthorpe, which was home to 50 and 61 Squadrons of Bomber Command. The site of the station has been hugely developed, but memorials and reminders abound in the area. For a greater detailing of memorials and mementoes in the Skellingthorpe area, see *Air Force Memorials of Lincolnshire*, by Mike Ingham, published by Midland Publishing.

'The Hero' at Overy Staithe, Norfolk, shows Lord Nelson who was born in a local vicarage. In 1963 the sign was replaced by a portrait of Wing Commander Guy Gibson vc of 'Dam Busters' fame, but local objections caused the admiral to be re-instated. The sign for 'The Ladybower' near Ashopton, Derbyshire shows

Above: *Plaque on the wall of 'The Wild Life', built on the site of the former RAF Skellingthorpe, near Lincoln.* Mike Ingham

Below: *A 'watering hole' for personnel from RAF Spilsby, 'The Bell' at Halton Holegate marks the connection in vivid terms with the sign showing a Lancaster flying over the pub.* Chris Salter

Battle of Britain Memorial Flight Lancaster I PA474 down low over Derwent Water, lining up on the towers of the Ladybower dam in 1993, in the same manner as the 'Lancs' of 617 Squadron practised 50 years before. Alan Curry

The pub sign of the 'Ladybower Inn' features the 617 Squadron badge and a Lancaster flying over the reservoir. The pub itself looks directly down on Derwent Water. Ken Ellis

a Lancaster in flight over Derwent Water and the 617 Squadron badge. No 617 Squadron used the local reservoir for practice runs in preparation for the dams raid. The back of the pub's menu explains the part played by the dam in the training of 617 and the menu itself includes 'Dambuster' steaks!

South of Grimsby, the A16 runs to the west of the village of Holton-le-Clay and over what was the eastern perimeter track of RAF Grimsby. Here can be found 'The Jug and Bottle' with an excellent painting of a Lancaster of the same name and its crew. 'The Jug and Bottle' was a Lancaster of 100 Squadron who were stationed at Grimsby from December 1942 to April 1945 and a certificate inside the pub declares that it was built on the site of one of 100 Squadron's dispersals. There are

'The Jug and Bottle' named after a Lancaster that once stood at dispersal near the site of the pub, Holton-le-Clay, Lincs. Mike Ingham

many other photographs and artefacts showing the connection. Mk I Lancaster PA177 (from the same batch as the RAF Battle of Britain Memorial Flight's airworthy PA474) was coded 'HW-J^2' ('Jig Two') and served only with 100, surviving through to being struck off charge on 20th December 1945, so the 'Jug and Bottle' was a lucky craft for her crews.

The village of Seaton Ross, East Yorkshire, lies just to the south of Melbourne, the bomber station mostly linked with 10 Squadron, who flew Handley Page Halifaxes from there 1942-45. In the village 'The Blacksmith's Arms' was the station's 'watering hole' and 10 Squadron made it very much their own. In the 1980s, the pub changed its name and has become one of the most famous of aeronautical pubs (even if it does not open at lunch time!) – 'The Bombers'.

Within the pub is what can only be described as a shrine, the amount of memorabilia and frame photographs is breathtaking. The ceiling of the main bar comes from wing and spar sections of de Havilland Mosquitoes. The bar itself was previously to be found serving in a similar capacity at the Officer's Mess at Melbourne.

This collection of artefacts is looked after by the 10 Squadron Association, currently under the custodianship of secretary Doug Dent. Once a month, the Association stages a Luncheon Club at 'The Bombers' after which they may well take a drive past their former airfield and then continue to Elvington and the Yorkshire Air Museum, where they can see progress on the Halifax recreation the museum has embarked upon. The pub sign depicts three 10 Squadron Halifax (with 'ZA-' codes) flying through a star-filled night with a quarter moon.

Other contemporary Bomber Command terminology incorporated into pub names are 'The Flarepath' at Hatfield, South Yorkshire, near the former RAF Lindholme, and 'The Pathfinder' at Maltby, near Rotherham, South Yorkshire. The sign displays the force's badge and the motto 'We Guide to Strike'. There is also a 'Pathfinder Hotel' in Leeds, West Yorkshire.

An undertaking followed by many who found themselves in enemy hands 'for the duration' was commemorated by 'The Escape', a pub that could be found close by Euston Station in London. The pub was renamed but the sign has been preserved by the RAF Escaping Society and is on public display amid the Society's display at the Lincolnshire Aviation Heritage Centre, East Kirkby.

The 'Ops Room' at the former RAF Portreath, Cornwall is, as its name suggests, a converted wartime building complete with mock control tower. Its lovely sign shows a Spitfire in flight carrying the codes 'D-B', those used by Douglas Bader (and on the pub sign at Tangmere, West Sussex).

The 'Ops Room' at Portreath, Cornwall, uses an airfield building and gives the impression of a watch tower. The pub sign is a Spitfire carrying the personalised marks of Douglas Bader, 'D-B'. Paul Shaw

The 'Owl and Crescent' at Calshot, Hampshire, was not readily recognisable as an aeronautical connection but it is taken from the badge of one of the squadrons based at the historic flying-boat station. Its 'Schneider Bar' also had mementoes of the pre-war seaplane races.

A wartime myth is the idea for 'The Gremlin' at Brecon, Powys. Unfortunately, the sign shows a pixie sitting on a toadstool in the moonlight rather than on an aircraft.

'The Guinea Pig' at East Grinstead, Sussex, is a commemoration of the nearby hospital specialising in plastic surgery, mainly for aircrew. The sign shows a winged pig descending in flames against the background of a crippled Spitfire.

It is fortunate that brewers often take note of their customers, as evidenced by the proposal to name a new hotel on the site of the old Clifton aerodrome at York 'The Memphis Belle'. It had no local relevance but after a brief stand the brewery gave in to what they admitted was 'the sheer depth of feeling from a number of people'. It is now called 'The Flying Legends' and the sign features the Handley Page Halifax and Westland Lysander which once flew from Clifton.

'Theme' pubs have become well established and some have had quite large budgets devoted to their 'fitting' out. One such case is 'The Meridian Bar and Grill' within the Meridian Business Park at the junction of the M69 and M1 west of Leicester. This is an American-style bar/diner and the

The Flying Fortress dominates the bar at 'The Meridian'. Examples of nose-art past and present are on show all over the pub. Ken Ellis

theme chosen is nose-art and a large number of photographs of nose-art old and new adorn the walls. Dominating the bar is a huge replica of a Boeing B-17 Flying Fortress. Perhaps about half-size, it features the famous Betty Grable swimsuit pose on the nose and the words *That Jones Boy!* While the purists may not like the camouflage scheme (or some of the B-17's contours), they will definitely object to the codes, 'LL-E' relate to a B-17F of the 91st Bombardment Group, 401st Bombardment Squadron, based at Kimbolton while the 'Triangle C' on the fin denotes the 303rd Bombardment Group, who lived at Molesworth! It is still an impressive sight. The barstaff were of the opinion that the management were going to change the 'theme' by late 1996, so the mock-up's days may be numbered!

The sign of 'The Chequers' near the former wartime fighter base at Fowlmere, Cambridgeshire, is adorned with the chequered design once applied to the 339th Fighter Group's P-51 Mustangs and 89 Squadron's Spitfires. The RAF unit's pale blue chequers are shown on one side of the pub sign, along with the note that No 19 flew Spitfires in 1940 (and 1941) when they alternated with the adjacent Duxford. The 339th carried red and white checkers (in their case) on their P-51Bs and later 'Ds, flying from Fowlmere from April 1944 for 12 months. The other side of the sign at 'The Chequers' declares this association.

Blue and white chequers as worn by 89 Squadron at 'The Chequers', Fowlmere. Fred Cubberley

Close to the site of Mount Farm aerodrome in Oxfordshire, 'The Berinsfield Arms' pub sign bears a Spitfire and Lockheed Lightning, types which once flew from the airfield. Although a variety of types flew from Mount Farm, it became famous as a home of photo-reconnaissance (PR) flying. The RAF's 140 Squadron flying from there with Spitfires until March 1943 when the USAAF unit which would become the 7th Photograph Group, moved in. The choice of a 'bomber nose' Lightning on the pub sign shows good research as the P-38 Lightning dedicated PR variants, the F-4 and the F-5, also flew from Mount Farm.

Short 'C-Class' flying-boat Canopus *taking off from the Medway, 1936. The 'boat gave its name to a Rochester pub in 1938.* Shorts

FAMOUS AIRCRAFT

Aircraft names with local associations are a popular choice. Near Filton, Gloucestershire, are 'The Bristol Bulldog' and 'The Pegasus', the latter is named after the Bristol engine. (There is also a 'Pegasus' near Liverpool Airport, Merseyside, but with the usual flying horse connotation, a reminder that all is not what it may seem.)

A more mundane Bristol product is remembered in 'The Wayfarer' at Southmead, near Filton, Gloucestershire. This was the all-passenger version of the Bristol Type 170 Freighter and the pub sign's artist put the 'registration' letters 'COUR' on the port wing and 'AGE' on the port to note the brewery and not as an aside to

the B.170's nickname – 'The Frightener'.

A famed engine of the Second World War is the subject of 'The Merlin' at Pinkney Green, near Maidenhead. It was opened in 1979 near a housing estate which has many of its roads named after wartime aircraft. There was another 'The Merlin' in Derby, home of Rolls-Royce.

'The Canopus' at Rochester, Kent, opened in 1938, acts as a reminder of the many flying-boats built by Shorts and flown from the River Medway. G-ADHL *Canopus* was the prototype Short S.23 'C-Class' flying-boat, which flew for the first time on 4th July 1936. *Canopus* was scrapped on the River Hythe in 1947 and one of its control wheels was presented to the pub.

'The Flying Boat' at Pembroke Dock in Dyfed is one of the Short Sunderland's spiritual homes. It is a pity that 'The Flying Boat's' sign is looking a little weathered, an ever present problem with pub signs. The time for a repaint is often the time when the brewery decides to rename the pub! There are other 'Flying Boats' at Poole, Dorset, and Calshot, Hampshire, and there was one at Felixstowe, Suffolk, all marine bases at one time. The original sign from 'The Flying Boat' at Calshot, a Sunderland overflying a convoy, is now displayed at the Museum of D-Day Aviation at Shoreham Airport, West Sussex. The pub was the wartime Officers' Mess for the base.

'The Sunderland Flying Boat' at Sunderland, Tyne & Wear, distinguishes itself by being bereft of anything to show what its namesake looks like! At The Hoe in Plymouth there is 'The Walrus', after the Supermarine amphibian. There was another 'Walrus' at Lowfield Heath, near Gatwick Airport, which is believed to have been named after the 'Shagbat'.

For centuries inn-keeping was almost a traditional occupation for retired servicemen and it is not uncommon today. At Mewlyn, Cornwall, the landlord, a former Fleet Air Arm pilot, has called his pub 'The Swordfish'. The sign has the fish on one side and the aircraft on the other. There is another 'Swordfish' at Lee-on-Solent, Hampshire, (with a 'Taranto Bar') on the edge of the airfield from which they once flew. There is also a 'Wyvern' at Lee, named after Westland's problematical naval fighter. The 'Fairey Firefly' at Hayes, Greater London, remembered a type which was produced in a nearby factory. The sign, which depicted an 'interestingly' camouflaged Firefly of the AS.6 ilk, was unveiled by Gordon Slade, former chief test pilot for Fairey.

The original sign for 'The Flying Boat' public house at Calshot, Hants, is preserved at the Museum of D-Day Aviation at Shoreham Airport, West Sussex. The building was used as an Officers' Mess and is said to be haunted.
Ken Ellis

The sign for 'The Flying Lancaster' is preserved in an out-house of what is now the 'The Lancaster Arms' at Desford, Leics. Dave Smith

'The Flying Lancaster' at Desford, Leicestershire, was originally 'The Lancaster Arms' but the name was changed by a landlord who was a former Lancaster pilot. Presumably when he retired his successor reverted to the old name which refers to the land being owned by the Duchy of Lancaster and the current pub sign is dominated by the red rose of Lancashire. Fortunately the aircraft signboard still exists in an outbuilding. It features a Lancaster caught in searchlights and more than a little challenged by perspective! The code letters worn, 'DI-G', don't relate to a Lancaster unit.

In similar vein, at Morden, Surrey, can be found the 'Beverley' which did exhibit a pub sign of the famous Blackburn Beverley transport aircraft. The publican of the time being former 'Bev' aircrew but the name (if not the sign) lives on!

Woodford, south of Manchester was where the very first Avro Lancaster made its first flight on 9th January 1941 and many of the illustrious breed were built there. Today, those who work at what is now Avro International Aerospace, building the RJ series of airliners, can relax at 'The Lancaster Club' close to the main entrance. The large sign is graced by two Lancasters carrying 44 Squadron ('KM-') codes along with Theakston's Seal of the Official of the Peculier of Masham c 1741. (Over at Warton, Lancashire, the British Aerospace Military Aircraft Division has a similar undertaking, 'The Lightning Club' - see under 'Planes and Pints'.

There are many other pubs which have taken the names of aeroplanes for various reasons. 'The Spitfire' at Thornaby-on-Tees, Cleveland, is on the site of the old RAF station. Sadly, in a recent refurbishment all aviation photographs were removed.

At Hastings, East Sussex, 'The Wellington' has the aircraft on its sign because an Initial Training Wing for wartime aircrew was sited close by. The main subject of the pub sign was an 'AA'-coded 'Wimpey', denoting 75 Squadron. One wonders if there is a connection, or was this a picture on hand to help the artist? A Vickers Warwick aircraft is depicted on the sign of 'The Warwick' in Warwick Avenue, Woodbridge, Suffolk

Several 'Tiger Moths' include one in Bedford and another in Manchester

here was another, now long gone, at Cranoe Moor, Barnsley, South Yorkshire. Most famous is the one in Chatham, overlooking Rochester aerodrome in Kent, whose sign was unveiled in 1959 from the cockpit of a Tiger which had been wheeled on to the Maidstone-Chatham road! The chap doing the unveiling being Colonel 'Mossy' Preston of the Royal Aero Club.

Another famous de Havilland design, the 1930s DH.88 Comet racer, is commemorated at Hatfield, Hertfordshire, by 'The Comet Hotel' to the south of the now-closed Hatfield airfield. A pleasing example of late-1930s architecture, its model Comet is poised on top of a rather strange 'totem pole', the work of the distinguished sculptor Eric Kennington.

'The Flying Fortress' opened in December 1988 on the edge of the former 8th Air Force airfield of Rougham, Suffolk. The refurbished building was previously a farm manager's house and during the war was taken over as the headquarters of a USAAF ground unit. The car park is part of the old perimeter track.

On one side of the pub sign is a B-17 Flying Fortress in cartoon form. It is painted on what appears to be aircraft alloy, complete with rivet holes. The other side has a more formal view of a B-17 and both aircraft bear the 'Square A' marking of the local 94th Bomb Group. Within the pub can be found a lot of memorabilia on the airfield.

'The Comet Hotel' has a model of the de Havilland DH.88 Comet racer G-ACSS Grosvenor House *displayed on a plinth in the car park.* Ken Ellis

Helicopters are represented by 'The Chopper Arms' close to the busy Army Air Corps base at Middle Wallop, Hampshire, and 'The Chopper' near Battersea Heliport in London. The latter is current.

Near Hendon, 'The Hind and Hart' recalls two Hawker aircraft types which once flew from the former RAF station – now the site of the RAF Museum.

AIRPORTS AND AIRLINERS

Airports are a common source of pub names and, in the case of some long closed, they are a form of memorial. Examples were 'The Aerodrome' at Waddon, close to the old Croydon Airport and 'The Propeller' in the same district.

'The Old Airport Inn' at Tremorfa, South Glamorgan, had a sign with a biplane flying over the original Cardiff Municipal Airport, which opened in 1931 with the wonderful name Splott. (This was a nearby village now consumed in the sprawl of Cardiff but itself remembered in the Splottlands district of the city!) The title Pengam Moors was adopted from around 1936. The present-day sign is of Spitfire V AB910 wearing the codes 'QJ-J' of 92 Squadron. AB910 is, of course, one of the Spitfires with the Battle of Britain Memorial Flight, presently based at Coningsby Lincolnshire. The aircraft wore this markings from the late 1950s to the mid-1960s and again from 1973 to 1978. No.92 Squadron did have brief South Welsh connections, flying Spitfire Is from Pembrey near Llanelli in the summer of 1940

At delightful Swansea Airport (Fairwood Common) within the base of the control tower in the 'Spitfire Bar and Grill which is suitably decorated with Spitfire photographs. Spitfires did indeed grace the airfield, but it was largely the domain of Mosquitoes. A grandstand view of the comings and goings of the light aircraft population can be had from the picnic area.

Spitfire V AB910 (G-AISU), then operated by Vickers, at a display in the late 1950s and wearing the 92 Squadron markings 'QJ-J'. This machine is now a part of the Battle of Britain Memorial Flight and features on the pub sign of 'The Old Airport' at Tremorfa, South Glamorgan. MAP

In north Wales, Caernarfon Airport, the former RAF Llandwrog and birthplace of the Mountain Rescue Service, boasts The Dakota Restaurant'. Dakotas were never a major part of the airfield's wartime scenery but they are to be seen occasionally visiting these days. Operated by Air Caernarfon, which part of The Atlantic Group, the Dakotas of Air Atlantique, particularly those of the Marine Pollution Control Unit, make practice approaches and have been known to drop in for a longer stay.

The 'Happy Landings' in Bristol first showed a Britannia in the early 1970s and then a Bristol helicopter but in 1982 the design was altered to a safely landed parachutist. It is near the old Whitchurch airport that served Bristol before 1939. More appropriately, it recalls the Bristol Aeroplane Company at Filton and the current image on the pub sign is of a Beaufighter TT.10 target tug. There was another 'Happy Landings' at Stanwell, in the vicinity of Heathrow. In the early 1970s, the sign included a dramatic 'nose-on' view of a jetliner thundering down a runway.

Bristol and the surrounding area seems to have more than its fair share of aeronautical pubs. At Patchway is 'The Britannia' with a pub sign commemorating the famous 'Whispering Giant' airliner that was built at nearby Filton. Difficult to categorise, but well worthy of inclusion somewhere in this work is the 'Mill House' in

'Happy Landings', near to Bristol's original airport of Whitchurch. The sign, a Beaufighter TT.10 commemorates aircraft production at Filton. Rod Priddle

Filton. This really should be a 'watering hole' but it is a brand new restaurant/pub and does not seem to be a particular 'haunt' of British Aerospace or Rolls-Royce workers, both having their plants within sight of the pub. Either way, the pub includes in its decor a huge number of frame photographs of Bristol-built and Rolls-Royce-powered aircraft – including examples in the loos!

There was another 'Britannia' at Stanwell, Middlesex, depicting the airliner in BOAC colours, which served Heathrow,

'The Britannia' is a popular name for a pub, but currently only the one in Patchway, Bristol, is concerned with the superb airliner. Series 312 G-AOVT of BOAC – now preserved by the Duxford Aviation Society. Jerome Knight

not far away. There are many other 'Britannias' to be found in the country, but they all allude to the lady to be found on the back of coins.

Leicester's pre-war airport at Braunstone is only a memory but it is kept alive by 'The Airmans', a delightful 1930s building in the style of an airport terminal of that era. It is run by Everards, a local brewing family, one of whose members was Sir Lindsey Everard. He was a prominent personality in pre-war light aviation and owned the private aerodrome at Ratcliffe, to the north of Leicester which was later taken over by Air Transport Auxiliary. The official name of the pub is 'The Airmans Rest', but this no longer appears on any of the pub signs except through the painting which is of three Irvin-clad pilots at rest in front of what might be a Gloster Gauntlet or Gladiator. Alongside the pub is the 'Jets' night-club.

Above: *Pilots at rest in front of a Gauntlet or Gladiator, on the sign for 'The Airmans', Braunstone, Leicester.*
Opposite: *'The Airmans', close to the site of Leicester's pre-war airport, was styled on the lines of an airport terminal.*
Both Dave Smith

Across the airfield from Bembridge Airport, Isle of Wight, is 'The Propeller Inn'. The somewhat utilitarian building is an adaptation of an building once used by Britten Norman in the heyday of BN-2 Islander production. As well as the metal propeller on the outside wall a vintage wooden prop adorns the bar and the aviation atmosphere is supported by a variety of prints and photographs.

Gloucestershire Airport at Staverton had its own pub, 'The Red Baron' which featured the fighter ace's Fokker Dr.I triplane on the pub sign. Alas it is no more...

'The Viscount' at Renfrew recalled Glasgow's original airport, now built over.

'The Red Baron' flew over Staverton Airport, Glos. Rod Priddle

'The Runway' at Bucksburn refers to the nearby Aberdeen Airport. At Fife Airport, Glenrothes, the recently-opened bar and restaurant glories under the name of 'The Tipsy Nipper'! Many will be the drinker and diner who does not realise that it is not a description of the potential state of its patrons, but in honour of the diminutive single-seat sportsplane designed by Belgian Ernest Oscar Tips in 1957!

Less imaginative are several 'Airports' including one only yards from the holding point for Runway 24 at Manchester and another near Gloucestershire Airport. The Manchester version has a fine painting of a British Airways Concorde as its motif. Manchester's first airport was at Barton, where there is still a thriving light aircraft

aerodrome. The 'Airport Hotel' at Barton has a charming pub sign, depicting an airman holding a frothing pint standing in front of a Sopwith-like biplane fighter. To the east of Bristol Airport at Felton is the 'Airport Tavern' which is graced with a 1930s-style painting of what could loosely be called a Handley Page HP.42 standing outside an airport terminal building that could *only* be Croydon!

On the southern perimeter of Gatwick Airport, near Charlwood House, is the 'Flight Tavern' a large pub set in extensive grounds, overlooking the airport. It affords excellent views of activity and on a summer's day, a pint, a platter and a zoom lens will produce an excellent afternoon. The pub sign is interesting considering

Concorde adorns the sign of 'The Airport' at Manchester. Dave Smith

A 'Sopwith' of sorts can be found on the 'Airport Hotel' at Barton. Paul Shaw

..ristol's 'Airport Tavern' looks more like Croydon! Ken Ellis

the tavern's immediate surroundings, it depicts a gas balloon and a 'Sopwith'. A pub at Horley, Surrey, is named 'The Gatwick' after the airport.

Airport bars and lounges are sometimes given suitable aviation names. 'The Blenheim Lounge' and 'Lancaster Restaurant' at Liverpool and Manchester Airports, respectively, recall the wartime aircraft built nearby. The 'Sanderling Bar' at Glasgow Airport is a reminder that Abbotsinch was once a Royal Naval Air Station, HMS *Sanderling*.

Recently refurbished, the interior of 'The Aviator Hotel' at Northampton's delightful Sywell aerodrome offers views of the aircraft parking area and has a wide variety of artefacts on show, most of which relate to Sywell's crowded history. Dominating the central area is a glass case holding a Spitfire instrument panel and control stick.

While overlooking the comings and goings of Airbuses and Boeings, the 'Flight Tavern' at Charlwood chooses another era for its pub sign. Ken Ellis

*Top: Britain's first jet, the Gloster
E.28/39 takes to the air for the first time,
from Cranwell, Lincs, 15th May 1941.
Three pubs celebrate the aircraft and Sir
Frank Whittle.* Rolls-Royce

*Above: The 'Sir Frank Whittle' at
Lutterworth, Leics, depicts the man and
the engine.* Dave Smith

JET AGE

The pioneer of the jet engine is the inspiration for the 'Sir Frank Whittle' which stands a few hundred yards from the site at Lutterworth, Leicestershire, where he ran his first jet engine. To be found within are the 'Meteor Restaurant' and 'The E.28 Lounge' with a model of the first British jet aeroplane, the Gloster E.28/39. The pub sign is a formal portrait of Whittle, in RAF uniform with one of his engines in the background.

There are two 'Jet and Whittles', at Lower Tuffley, Gloucestershire, the other at Leamington Spa, Warwickshire. Lower Tuffley's example includes a portrait of Whittle and of the Gloster E.28/39 which was built (but not flown) at nearby Hucclecote. In the early 1970s, the Leamington example showed a dramatically-posed E.28/39 and a cross-section of the engine. 'The Jet' at Oxhey, Herts, had a de Havilland Sea Vixen on its board. This was

Left: *The 'Jet and Whittle' at Lower Uffley, Glos, shows the man and the 28/39.* Rod Priddle

replaced by steeply climbing delta-wing that closest approximated to the Avro 07, or Fairey Delta 2.

Apart from the previously mentioned balloon', Lutterworth also has the 'Red Arrow' on the road to the former Bitteswell airfield where the team's aircraft were once overhauled by British Aerospace. This pub, built in the 1960s, started life with the then trendy name 'The Flying Saucer'! (Its current name is much more accurate, at least from an architectural point of view, the building being triangular in shape!)

There are several 'Concordes' including one at Ilkeston, Nottinghamshire, but the most appropriate is in Bristol. 'The Double-O-Two' at Yate, is not far from Filton where the second prototype (the

Initially called 'The Flying Saucer', the pub on the Bitteswell Road, Lutterworth, was hardly the right shape! Renamed as the 'Red Arrow', the pub sign carries a Hawk T.1 of the team. Both Ken Ellis

Above: *'Batting in' Concorde 002 G-BSST on its last flight in Yeovilton, Somerset, 26th July 1976 for preservation by the Fleet Air Arm Museum and Science Museum. The 'Double-O-Two' at Yate, Glos, remembers the aircraft.* FAAM

Below: *The Rolls-Royce 'Flying Bedstead' (or Thrust Measuring Rig) made its first flights from Hucknall, Notts, in August 1954. A pub nearby is named after the strange device.* Rolls-Royce

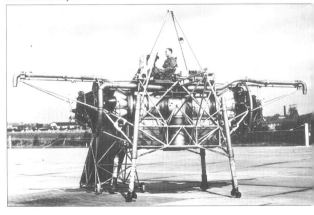

rst British-flown example) made its first light. It was opened in 1971 by BAC's eputy chief test pilot John Cochrane.

In London, 'The Jumbo Jet' in SW5 lay eneath the flight path for Heathrow, vhich is well used to the sight and sound f 747s. At Wolverhampton, West Midands, 'The Pilot' depicts a jet pilot, all kited up. This is as good a time as any to varn that there are many 'Pilots' in the ountry, the bulk of them being close to orts and rivers and relating to the nautial variety!

Buccaneers were built at Brough, near lull, and there is a pub of this name neary. Hucknall, near Nottingham, was the cene of the early vertical take-off trials, ne local 'Flying Bedstead' being appropritely named. Also at Hucknall is a 'Harrir'. Strictly speaking the powerplant for

the Harrier was the Bristol Siddeley (now Rolls-Royce) Pegasus and a product of Filton, not Derby.

'The Harrier' at Hamble, Hampshire, owes its name and sign to the fact that parts for the aircraft were built locally. At Melksham, Wiltshire, on part of what was the former RAF Melksham, is a new pub also called 'The Harrier' with a Sea Harrier FRS.1 illustrated on the pub sign. There is no readily apparent local connection with the Harrier, naval or otherwise. RAF Melksham, a non airfield technical training school, closed in 1964.

Another 'Harrier' can be found at Gunthorpe, Peterborough, Cambridgeshire. It lies directly under the eastern approach to RAF Wittering – home of the RAF's UK-based Harriers. The reverse of the sign shows the feathered variety. (Within the

Previously named 'The Bird', the pub at Brampton, Cambridgeshire, is now 'The Harrier'. The sign also shows the bird of prey of the same name. Bill Taylor

Clockwise: 'The Harrier' at Brampton, Cambridgeshire, the reverse carries a portrait of the bird of prey. Bill Taylor A rendition of a Sea Harrier FRS.1 adorns the pub sign of Melksham's 'The Harrier'. Rod Priddle 'The Harrier' at Gunthorpe, near Peterborough is another that shares its sign with a Harrier GR.3 and a fine depiction of the feathered version. Both Bill Taylor

The superb Harrier 'jump-jet' has been 'adopted' by several public houses, some with geographic and historic connections with the aircraft, others less so. RAF GR.5 illustrated. Alan Curry

...own of Stamford, Lincolnshire, just north of Wittering, can be found a pub referred to by locals as 'The Harrier'. Despite the nearby aeronautical association, the pub is more fully named 'The Marsh Harrier' in honour of the bird of prey, *Circus Aerugiposus!* Another warning to think laterally when it comes to pub names!) At Brampton, Cambridgeshire can also be found another, recently-renamed 'Harrier' having previously been 'The Bird'. Like the Gunthorpe one, this pub sign carries a Harrier GR.3 on one side and the raptor on the other.

An attractive subject on a sign at Merthyr Tydfil, Glamorgan, is an Avro Vulcan in its early anti-nuclear flash white fin-ish, for 'The Vulcan Inn'. While South Wales may not strike the reader immediately as Vulcan 'territory', nearby RAF St Athan, was a centre for the type's maintenance. Manchester was the birthplace of the Vulcan and it is not surprising that a pub carries that name here also. At Buckhurst Hill, Essex, is the 'B-52 Bar' named after the awesome eight-jet bomber, the Boeing Stratofortress.

MISCELLANY

Pub mementoes of women's contributions to aviation are few but 'The Flying Eagle', appropriately in Mollison Way, Edgware, on the site of the old Stag Lane aerodrome, honours Amy Johnson. More general was 'The Air Hostess' in Harmondsworth, not far from Heathrow, and another of the same name near Tollerton aerodrome, Nottingham. The latter is not very relevant since the site is little more than a centre for private flying.

Becoming quite an enigma as the research for this book continued was the 'Turn and Slip', a pub sign espied at Wroxham, amid the Norfolk Broads, the local pubs being 'The King's Head' at Hoveton and 'The Castle' at Wroxham. It seems that the inn sign, based upon the aircraft instrument was 'pub-less' (there is an increasing trade in pub signs, sadly including poor and over-priced 'repros' made almost to order) but deserves tracking down to its origins.

Aircraft carriers were represented by 'Invincible' at Portsea, Hampshire, and 'Eyres Monsell', Leicester. Although the second has the carrier on its sign, it is said to be named after the battle cruiser of 1914 vintage. There was an 'Ark Royal' at Devonport and an 'Eagle' at Dereham, Norfolk, the second inspired by the ship built in 1946 to replace the original which was torpedoed in 1942. There is another at Plymouth with the carrier on one side of the sign and the bird on the other.

Moving on to the space age, apart from the now re-named 'Flying Saucer' at Lutterworth, there is one of the same title at Gillingham, Kent and in Liverpool, the 'Man in the Moon' at Cambridge and elsewhere and 'The Astronaut' at Stockton-on-Tees, Cleveland. 'The Early Bird' in Nottingham, refers to the communications satellite launched in 1965 as well as the proverbial bird; both appear on the sign. Another satellite is the theme for 'The Telstar' at Billingham, Tees-side.

Names which defy categorisation were 'The Catch 22' in London NW11, named after Joseph Heller's famous novel loosely based (very!) on the US Army Air Force in Italy and 'The Silver Bullet' in London N4 which commemorates a combined rail/air London to Paris race.

WATERING HOLES

Where air
and ground crew`
tried to forget there was
a war on...

WHAT IS A 'WATERING HOLE'?

Many of the pubs mentioned in the first chapter will, of course, have been 'watering holes' in their own right, most probably under a previous name. However, this chapter is devoted to the pubs that during the Second World War would have been jammed with airmen and airwomen, often spilling out into the road. Every airfield had one or more local pubs to which its personnel would repair at every available opportunity – these were the 'watering holes'. Some pubs still serve in this capacity to nearby Royal Air Force, Fleet Air Arm and Army Air Corps airfields.

It is the 'watering hole' that takes much more sleuthing to find. They will not necessarily have aeronautical names, though as we have seen, they may well have been renamed post-war to confirm their association. With the majority not having an obvious aviation connection more local research is required to find them. The effort is often worth it for many pubs have displays showing the local station (or base in USAAF parlance) and many contain much more personal memorabilia. In some, while there may be no trace of their past, the atmosphere may well be sufficient, particularly if it is known that a well known 'name' frequented the 'hole'.

In many such pubs comfort was distinctly lacking, most with stone floors and wooden benches. As late as the 1960s, one of the writers (!) recalls the somewhat basic country pubs of East Anglia, apparently unchanged since the war!

To establish the 'watering holes' of an airfield a working knowledge of the area is needed. Not every pub in every village will have been frequented, there will have been favourites, and these will have varied within the ranks. The closest pub to the main gate need not have been the 'watering hole' to be seen in (drunk or otherwise!) and there are several cases mentioned here where several pubs must have been *passed* to get to the favoured one.

There were many more pubs in operation in 1939-45 than in the closing years of the millennium! While investigating which was the favourite pub, bear in mind that it may have changed its name, become a private house or been demolished! Locals can also have their memories play tricks and talk of 'where did the Spitfire pilots go after a battle?' may produce the answer of the name of 'the local' because that is fixated in their mind when they mean the pub that *used* to be 'the local' before the latest!

Examples of mementoes include *Luftwaffe* target photograph which just happens to show the pub! Another painting of a fighter pilot from the local airfield. It is sad that they often disappear over the years for various reasons. Modern 'theme' pubs have a tendency, as aviation writer Mike Jerram very aptly commented, to acquire memorabilia 'by the yard' with no feel for the subject.

FIGHTER HAUNTS

A handful of pubs have become virtual shrines to wartime fliers, the most famous being 'The White Hart' at Brasted, a few miles from Biggin Hill. A black-out screen scrawled with the signatures of dozens of Battle of Britain pilots and their successors has been preserved. The full story can be found in *Inn of The Few*, written by wartime licensee Katherine Preston.

From the famous fighter airfield at Hawkinge, Kent, a small, narrow lane leads to the tiny village of Paddlesworth. Along here is the 'Cat and Custard Pot' a small pub that must have had elasticated walls. It was a famous haunt for fighter pilots from the airfield and it does not take much to imagine open-topped MGs hurtling down the lane, crowded with pilots and 'floozies'. Today, there is a lot of the original atmosphere, and the walls

At Paddlesworth, Kent, the 'Cat and Custard Pot' must have seen many an aerial battle re-enacted by pilots from Hawkinge. Ken Ellis

carry many aeronautical photos, most of them unconnected with the famous fighter station.

Travel west along the south coast from Hawkinge to Westhampnett, West Sussex. This is another famous fighter airfield, now partially the site of the motor racing circuit, but still a light airfield, although it now goes under the name of Goodwood. Douglas McRoberts' delightful book *Lions Rampant, The Story of 602 Spitfire Squadron* (William Kimber) sheds light on the station's 'watering holes'. No 602 (City of Glasgow) Squadron arrived at Westhampnett in August 1940, placing their Spitfire Is into the teeth of the Battle of Britain. They stayed until December 1940 and gave a very good account of themselves.

Such efforts naturally led to the need to unwind and the evenings found migrations to the local pubs. McRobert explains that 'The Dolphin' in Chichester were popular with the pilots, while the 'Green Dragon', also in Chichester, was the haunt of the aircraftsmen. There were others, further afield:

They had their favourite watering holes, too. 'The Victoria Hotel', Bognor, where Hilda Godsmark was one of the attractions, the 'Old Ship Inn' down at Bosham, where Sandy Johnstone found himself at the same table as the actor David Niven. It was a curious way to fight a war.

Bognor Regis is, of course, on the coast and offered a wide variety of attractions for the combatants. Bosham is

Just where did the lads go and unwind? Often to 'the city' but also to a 'local'. Spitfire V of 130 Squadron. via Alan Curry

delightful place in a cove that is part of the Chichester Harbour inlet, further to the west of the town.

Not so well known is the 'St Leonard's Hotel' at St Leonard's, Dorset, which has two vertical wall 'plaques' originally signed on the plaster surface and now covered with glass for preservation. They bear the signatures of airmen of many Allied nations who flew from Hurn, Ibsley and other aerodromes in the district.

Middle Wallop, Hampshire, now the home of army aviation, was a fighter station in the thick of the Battle of Britain fighting. A very popular haunt for pilots and groundcrew was the 'Six Bells' (or 'Six Clangers' as it was known locally) not in Middle Wallop, or Over Wallop, but to the south in Nether Wallop. One of the secrets of its attraction was that it could be reached from a crash gate on the southern perimeter, without the need to use the main gate. The pub was still a popular haunt up into the mid-1950s when it was used as an occasional billet.

A 'watering hole' loved by those old enough to have experienced it in wartime, fighter pilots based in the area since and those who just wished to take in the atmosphere is no more and a classic example of the frailty of things. This was the 'Three Horseshoes' close to RAF Coltishall in Norfolk. There was a large propeller blade on one of the external walls, alleged to have come from a Spitfire. Inside there were signatures on the

'The Fox' at Honington, Suffolk, was an obvious 'watering hole' for 12 Squadron when they were resident at the nearby RAF Station. The unit badge is a fox's head. Fred Cubberley

ceiling and traces of them on almost every flat surface, plus a host of artefacts. Alas it is no more – enjoy them while you can!

Another that has painted over the ceiling signatures is the 'George and Dragon' at Clyst St George, to the south of what is now Exeter Airport. RAF Exeter had a varied wartime career, being involved in several of the Channel Approaches battles. Crews 'adopted' the 'George and Dragon' and 'signed in' accordingly. Redecoration in the 1970s put an end to the wartime 'artwork'.

On the road into Padstow east of the village of St Merryn and north of the airfield of the same name is the 'Cornish Arms'. This was the first ward room of HMS *Vulture*, (RNAS St Merryn) and a display in the pub and a visitors book of former HMS *Vulture* (and HMS *Curlew*) personnel is kept.

Sometimes old names have been adapted to aeronautical and other modern themes. An example was 'The Fox' in Honington, Suffolk, whose signboard was inspired by 12 Squadron who have a fox's head as a badge. The unit worked up on HS Buccaneers at the base and it was an obvious venue for air and ground crew.

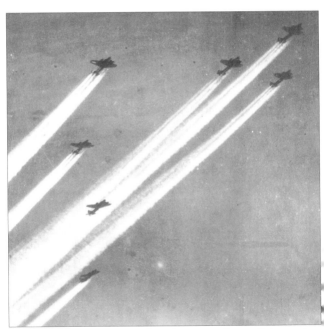

Bomber stations, by their very nature, housed many more aircrew, with increased demand on local 'watering holes'. B-17 Flying Fortresses trailing vapour en route to a target. Ken Ellis collection

BOMBER LAIRS

'The Eagle Hotel' in Cambridge was the bomber counterpart to 'The White Hart'. Clive James, the well-known television personality and author, had a room here for a while during his stay at the university. In the second volume of his autobiography he writes in his usual vivid fashion:

During the war, bomber crews from all over East Anglia had come to 'The Eagle' to spend, in hilarious conviviality, what was statistically likely to be one of their last evenings alive. Riding on each other's shoulders, into the deep red linoleum ceiling of the saloon they burned the numbers and nicknames of their squadrons with candle flames: a portent, doubly hideous for its innocence, of their own fate, and a grim token of the fiery nemesis they were bringing every night to the cities of Germany. To this day I can't enter that room without hearing their laughter, which becomes steadily more unmanning as I grow older. All my sons. Twenty years ago I was not all that much older than they had been when they were snuffed out. It was a hall of fame, a temple of the sacred flame, a trophy room for heroes.

Built in the 17th century, 'The Eagle Hotel' became a very popular venue for RAF and USAAF units scattered around Cambridge and writing names and units on the ceiling became very fashionable. During 1988, the pub was to close down, and a local, James Chainey, made considerable efforts to record all of the names written on the ceiling and starting to fade as the smoke of decades changed the colour of the ceiling. Elias Keen, writing in the June 1988 issue of *FlyPast* said:

A traditional pub in many respects, the last publican before the closure, John Wiseman, and the authorities at Corpus Christi College of Cambridge University, who own the site, were happy to help James in his quest to record all of the marks on the ceiling. Some of the inscriptions were easy to 'translate' and the units visiting the pub reflect the varied war effort undertaken in and around Cambridge. Other items took far more research. 'Bert's Boys' in a reference to 196 Squadron on Stirlings refers, of course, to 'Bomber' Harris, doyen of Bomber Command. Much more local was 'Bunty' – not a name on the side of a bomber, but a favourite barmaid of the time!

Two P-51 names, found in the smoke-encrusted paint were 'Tally-Ho' and 'Slender Tender'. 'The Old Stand-By' was the name of a B-17 of the 322nd Bombardment Squadron, Bassingbourn, piloted by James D Judy. It was lost on 9th October 1943 on a mission against Anklam and Marienburg with the loss of one life and nine made PoWs.

A place where 'writing on the wall' has survived is 'The Swan' at Lavenham, Suffolk. The hotel dates back to the 14th century and is a symphony of aged beams and arches – as is the small town. In one of the bars, safely protected behind a sheet of perspex is a small section of 'wattle and daub' in which a whole series of names have been inscribed. The local airfield opened in April 1944 with the arrival of the B-24 Liberators of the 487th Bombardment Group, who took on B-17 Flying Fortresses by the summer, and flew operations until the following July. There are photographs and other memorabilia to be seen in 'The Swan' and the proximity of nearby Wattisham (now an Army Air Corps station) is underlined with

a series of 'zaps' stuck around the bar!

Other favourite off-duty haunts for thousands of aircrew members were the 'Saracen's Head' in Lincoln, the 'George Hotel', Grantham, the 'White Hart' at Newark and 'Betty's Bar' in York. The York venue was originally a tavern but by 1939 it had become a cafe/restaurant and remains so to this day.

The 'Saracen's Head' (also known as 'The Snake Pit') became so well known that it was very much missed when it closed down in 1959. On 21st May 1993 a plaque was unveiled close to the site where the famed pub was to be found,

A famed 'watering hole', the 'Saracen's Head' in the centre of Lincoln closed in 1959 and today is a series of shops. The memorial plaque (circled) is on the building next door to the actual building. Mike Ingham

A plaque commemorating the 'Saracen's Head' is displayed nextdoor to where the famous pub stood.
Mike Ingham

noting that it was 'A favourite watering hole for thousands of RAF and Allied airmen and women who served in the Lincolnshire airfields'.

At Holme-on-Spalding Moor, East Yorkshire, 'Ye Olde Red Lion' was a favourite with aircrew from the station just to the south, and again from the late 1950s when Blackburns (later Hawker Siddeley and then British Aerospace) used the airfield for Buccaneer and Phantom development work.

Nestled in between the bomber airfields of Skipton-on-Swale and Topcliffe, west of Thirsk, is the 'Busby Stoop Inn'. It has displayed numerous relics relating to Skipton-on-Swale. Items included propeller blades and a seat made from a bomb casing.

Further south, Wickenby, Lincolnshire, was a famous bomber station. 'The White Hart' at Lissington to the north displays some of the more well-known photographs of the station in its heyday. 'The Turner Arms Hotel' to the south at Wragby was another favourite for personnel from Wickenby.

Ludford Magna gained fame as the home of 101 Squadron from 1943, pioneers in the art of deception thanks to the 'Airborne Cigar' (ABC) gear that their Lancasters carried. Two of the pubs in Ludford acted as watering holes for 101, the 'White Hart', which displays some Lancaster paintings, and the 'Black Horse'.

Just a stone's throw from the former RAF East Kirkby (now the Lincolnshire Aviation Heritage Centre) is the 'Red Lion Inn'. This was a haunt of both air and ground crew from the station. (As a rule, air and ground crews would adopt separate 'watering holes'.) At the end of a tour, aircrew carved their names in a table. The landlord has made sure the gnarled table has survived for other generations to experience.

'The Ship' at Brandon Creek, Norfolk, displays a photograph of the pub with signatures of 75 Squadron aircrew, including Sergeant James Ward vc who climbed out on the wing of a shot-up Wellington and

In Navenby, the 'Lion and Royal' remembers a special guest through the 'Gibson Room'. Ken Ellis

smothered the flames with an engine cover. This occurred on 7th July 1941 when New Zealander Ward was flying as second pilot in a Wellington I of No 75 on a raid to Münster out of Mildenhall, Suffolk. Ward's Victoria Cross was announced on 5th August 1941. Such was the lot of those who served Bomber Command that Ward did not have long to savour his award. His Wellington IC, X3205 of 75 Squadron, was hit by flak over Hamburg on 15th/16th September 1941. He and

three others of the crew were killed, the other two being taken prisoner.

The 'Lion and Royal' at Navenby, Lincolnshire, includes the 'Gibson Room' in memory of (then) Flight Lieutenant Guy Gibson, who was billeted there when he was stationed at RAF Digby, to the east. The pub includes a wide range of memorabilia and it is here that the (perhaps apocryphal) tale of Gibson's wedding night meal was enacted. The story goes that his crew wanted to give the couple something special and managed to 'find' a whole salmon. The precious fish was given to the publican and he was told to cook it for the Gibson's that evening. The newly weds were somewhat horrified to find that it had been deep fried in batter – the only way the publican knew how to cook fish! Across the road from the pub is the Navenby Heritage Room with plentiful exhibits of local history, including wartime flying.

North of Navenby on the A607 lies the famous bomber base of Waddington. The village of Waddington, lying but a short walk westwards from the main entrance to the base had a variety of 'watering holes' (remember there were many more pubs in those days than now!). Two survive and show off their proud links with the base through photographs and prints, the 'Horse & Jockey' and 'The Wheatsheaf'.

Air *and* ground crew from RAF Bottesford, 'adopted' 'The Reindeer' in nearby Long Bennington as a 'watering hole'. On the Great North Road, the pub also served as a convenient place to get lifts or be dropped off, heading for Newark, or down to Grantham. In those days, the A1 was far less formidable to cross than it is now!

The Society Friends of the Eighth (FOTE) has been responsible for small permanent displays of photographs and memorabilia in pubs and inns near former Eighth Air Force bases, which include the address of the contact within FOTE for that particular airfield. Researches are always continuing but some of the 'watering holes' of the 'Mighty Eighth' are given in the table.

Of the above, 'The Wheatsheaf Hotel' in Upper Benefield, near Oundle, Northamptonshire, was just down the road from the Flying Fortress base of Deenethorpe and the '401 Bar' within serves as an excellent reminder of this connection. The 401st Bomb Group operated from Deenethorpe from November 1943 to May 1945 – a long association with the locality. Within the '401 Bar' can be found a wide range of

'WATERING HOLES' OF THE EIGHTH AIR FORCE

Pub	Base	Unit
'Five Bells'	Rattlesden, Suffolk	447th Bomb Group
'King's Head'	Ridgewell, Essex	381st Bomb Group
'Pear Tree'	Bassingbourn, Cambridgeshire	91st Bomb Group
'Triple Plea'	Holton, Suffolk	489th Bomb Group
'Wheatsheaf'	Upper Benefield, Northamptonshire	401st Bomb Group
'The Woodman'	Nuthampstead, Hertfordshire	389th Bomb Group

Above: 'The Wheatsheaf Hotel' at Upper Benefield, Northants, which remembers the 401st BG from nearby Deenethorpe. Below: Part of the '401 Bar' inside 'The Wheatsheaf'. Both Ken Ellis

pictures (including a framed feature on the base from *FlyPast*), models and a display of artefacts dug up from the airfield.

Still in Northamptonshire and slipping a transport unit into the picture, in February 1944 the 315th Troop Carrier Group brought their Douglas C-47 Skytrains and Waco CG-4A Hadrian assault gliders into the newly-completed Spanhoe Lodge airfield. From here the group worked up in readiness for its part in D-Day and then prepared for the river crossings including the abortive Arnhem operation of September 1944. Down the hill in the Welland valley lay the village of Harringworth and it was to here that personnel came to slake their thirst.

The airfield took its name from a nearby farm and wood, because it was felt that 'Harringworth' was too close both phonetically and geographically to Harrington, near Market Harborough, home of the USAAF's 'Carpetbagger' units. Despite its official name, the airfield was known throughout the war at Harringworth or Wakerley, the two closest villages.

'The White Swan' in Harringworth celebrates the link with Spanhoe with a display of photographs, an airfield plan and colour profiles of the aircraft that flew from there. When built, the airfield cut the road link from Morcott to Deene, this provided a 'back route' from the northern dispersals and from here it was a short cycle to the other Spanhoe watering hole, 'The Exeter Arms' at Wakerley. From May 1945 the airfield was the domain of the RAF's 253 Maintenance Unit collecting and disposing of tens of thousands of military vehicles, and from then until late 1947 the airmen looking after this operation 'circuited' between Harringworth and Wakerley with forays to the 'George & Dragon' at Seaton.

Trans-Atlantic loyalties and connections were brought in when it looked as though 'The Blue Lion' at North Pickenham, Norfolk, was to close and be turned into a series of houses. A Grade II listed building, the owners expressed intentions to turn it into a private house and to build two more dwellings alongside. The local parish council objected and in Lexington, Kentucky, the 2nd Air Division Association brought its weight down on what was their favourite 'watering hole'. Thankfully, the plans came to nought and the pub lives on.

'The Blue Lion' is but a short distance from North Pickenham airfield, which was home to the 2nd AD's 491st and 492nd Bombardment Groups who flew B-24 Liberators. The bar carries plenty of mementoes from the 491st and 492nd and regular reunions are staged there.

Some pubs and hotels were actually requisitioned for the RAF. For example, the 'Petwood House Hotel' at Woodhall Spa, Lincolnshire was used from January 1944 as an Officers' Mess for the elite 617 Squadron based at the local airfield. To this day, the hotel proudly flies the RAF

The superb grounds and house that make up the 'Petwood House Hotel' at Woodhall Spa, Lincolnshire. Mike Ingham

The 'Dam Busters' bar within the 'Petwood House Hotel', including a plaque noting that the hotel served as the Officers' Mess for 617 Squadron 1943-45. Mike Ingham

ensign to mark this association. In the car park can be found the remains of a development 'inert' of the famous 'bouncing bomb'. As well as memorabilia inside the hotel, another attraction is the impressive 617 monument in the town centre, in the form of a breached dam.

Another Woodhall Spa watering hole is to be found south of both the town and the airfield, the 'Blue Bell Inn' at Tattershall Thorpe. This was, and still is, a favoured spot for RAF personnel. (The RAF still maintains an enclave on the former airfield site, used for testing RB.199 engines for Tornados from Coningsby.) There are many pictures within highlighting activities at Woodhall Spa, in particular of 617 and 627 Squadrons.

'The Baginton Oak' adjacent to Coventry Airport was commandeered as Station HQ until September 1941 when a purpose-built site was opened at RAF Honiley, the parent aerodrome.

MEMORIALS AND ENEMY ACTION

Memorials can be found in a few pubs, such as the propeller blade and plaque in memory of the crew of a Wellington which crashed close to 'The Lamb Inn' at Great Rissington, Gloucestershire. This was Mk I R1028 of 21 Operational Training Unit, which crashed on approach to nearby Little Rissington on the night of 7th October 1943. Five were killed in the crash, only Sergeant John Smith survived. In 1988 John Smith had a plaque erected in the pub, including the names of those who were killed as a memorial.

There is another Wellington prop blade at 'The Star Hotel', Pershore, Hereford and Worcester. It came from Mk III X3704 of 23 Operational Training Unit which crashed behind the pub during a 'Wings for Victory' flypast on 29th May 1943. All five on board were killed.

Huby Fairhead, tireless secretary of the Norfolk and Suffolk Aviation Museum (more of this in 'Planes and Pints') also spends much time chronicling the aviation history of East Anglia. His *Aeronautical Memorials of Norfolk* makes great reading and includes three incidents where pubs were 'on the receiving end'.

On 26th April 1941 the 'Ferry Inn' at Horning, Norfolk, took a direct hit which killed 22 people, including three pilots from RAF Coltishall. A plaque in the rebuilt pub describes the incident.

On 12th June 1942, the 'Eagle Hotel' in King's Lynn, Norfolk, was hit by one of four bombs dropped from a Dornier Do 217. Among the casualties inside the pub were five crew from a 115 Squadron Wellington, stationed at Marham, and an RAF AC2.

The 'Gallon Pot' near the market place in Great Yarmouth, Norfolk, has a stone built into a wall, that declares: *'The Gallon Pot', founded by W N Burroughs 1772, destroyed by enemy action 1943, rebuilt by E Lacon and Co 1959.*

Another wartime casualty was 'The Caernarvon Castle' in Birkenhead, Merseyside, which rose from the ashes many years later with appropriate commemorations.

On 29th July 1944, B-24H Liberator *My Momma Done Told Me* from the 490th Bombardment Group was returning from a mission to its home base at Eye, Suffolk with engine trouble. It hit a tree while on approach and crashed beside the Ipswich to Norwich (the present-day A140) in front of 'The Swan Inn' at Brome. Two of the crew died from their injuries.

PLANES & PINTS

Pubs, inns, night spots and aeroplanes!

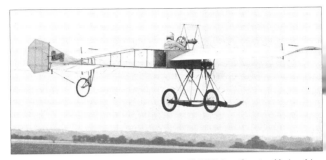

Ken Wallis flying the replica Wallbro monoplane (G-BFIP) from Swanton Morley. A bar in the 'Ambassador Hotel' at Norwich Airport commemorates the original.
Arrow Air Services

PLANES AND PINTS

While all pilots will agree that the 'throttle and bottle' should never be mixed, there have been cases were hostelries have displayed whole aircraft by way of attraction or association. In Britain there have been several attempts over the years to utilise redundant airliners or large military types as bars or restaurants. To date none of these have come to fruition, which is a pity as in Europe and the USA there are many such venues. Up until now, it has been a case of an aeroplane in the beer garden, or dangling from the roof in a night club, or, in the case of one aviation museum – a pub at the main entrance!

At Norwich Airport (once RAF Horsham St Faith) is the Stakis 'Ambassador Hotel'. 'The Wallbro Bar' gets its name from a monoplane built by the *Wall*is *bro*thers and flown from Reymerston Hall, Norfolk, in 1910. Powered by a 25hp JAP, the monoplane put Norfolk on the aircraft building 'map' not just because it was almost certainly the first designed and flown in the county, but also because it was one of the first in Britain to use steel tube construction, supplied by the firm of Accles and Pollock.

In 1972 K H and G Wallis decided to emulate their father and uncle and build a replica Wallbro, again ordering their tube from Accles and Pollock. Powered by a McCulloch 'flat-four' of 70hp, the replica did not fly from the family home at Reymerston Hall, but from Swanton Morley aerodrome, on 10th August 1978. The Wallis family still treasure the replica. K H Wallis is better known as Wing Commander Ken Wallis of autogyro fame and his most famous creation crops up later.

The hotel displays a variety of plaques and pictures within and outside in the forecourt is a full-size replica of a Spitfire V. This is painted in the colours of 64 Squadron, who flew from Horsham St Faith from August 1945 to August 1946, albeit with Mustang IVs.

Most spectacular of all, although not at an airport, is 'Dakota's American Bistro' at Fleet, Hampshire, which uses a Dakota fuselage as a centre-piece, along with many other Dakota components. Opened in April 1992, 'Dakotas' makes use of large chunks of C-47A N9050T acquired in a derelict state from the former Hal Safi airfield on Malta. During the opening period, the tail section of the 'Dak' was put into the nearby Fleet Pond, in a suitably

'crashed' mode. This served well as an attraction, but quickly became counter-productive as passing trains and even the occasional aircraft would report the 'ditching'! With an extensive American-style menu, 'Dakotas' has a vast amount of artefacts to look at, as well as the cockpit which dominates the bar area.

Amid the glamour and opulence at the 'Hilton' at Gatwick Airport can be found a very faithful replica of Amy Johnson's famed DH Gipsy Moth G-AAAH Jason. This 'flies' overhead of the central cafe-bar. It has been on display since 1980.

One pub offers much more than any other – it provides the gateway to a fascinating collection of aircraft and artefacts. This is 'The Buck' at Flixton, near Bungay,

Jason, *a very good replica of Amy Johnson's DH Moth in the foyer of the 'Hilton',* Gatwick Airport. Ken Ellis

Above: 'The Buck' at Flixton, 'gateway' to the Norfolk and Suffolk Aviation Museum, note the museum sign.
Below: A view of the museum; left to right Lightning, Canberra, Sea Prince, Valetta. Both Ken Ellis

Suffolk. Behind the pub is the superb Norfolk & Suffolk Aviation Museum and it has to be said that the two enterprises complement one another wonderfully! (The museum is open from Easter to October on Sundays and Bank Holidays, and also on Tuesdays, Wednesdays and Thursdays in July and August. More details in *Aviation Museum of Britain*, No.2 in our Pocket Guide series, see page 94.)

There have been public houses in the past that have succeeded in displaying aircraft. Landlord of the 'Queen's Head', in Allens Green, at Sawbridgeworth, Hertfordshire, in 1970 was former Hurricane pilot George Jackson. He acquired one of the full-size replicas used in the filming of the epic 'The Battle of Britain' and displayed the Hurricane in the car park. By 1974 the weather was taking its toll of the replica and in 1975 the Hurricane was towed away and eventually ended up on display in New Zealand.

Above: *Skeeter AOP.12 XL765 on show at the 'Swan at Pimlico', Leverstock Green, Hertfordshire, 1989.* Alan Allen

Below: *Plaything Hiller G-ARTG at the 'White Hart Inn', Stockbridge, Hampshire, in 1985.* Ken Ellis

Also in Hertfordshire, this time at Leverstock Green, the 'Swan at Pimlico' installed Percival Provost T.1 WW442 as an attraction in April 1987. By the following year it had been joined by SARO Skeeter AOP.12 XL765 and an anti-aircraft gun. By December 1991 both machines had gone.

Another pub that displayed a helicopter was the 'White Hart Inn' at Stockbridge, Hants. Acquired in 1982, Hiller UH-12C G-ARTG was used as both an attraction – 'parked' prominently on the corner of the pub and a kiddies plaything. The chopper was scrapped in the summer of 1986.

An aircraft of an entirely different ilk 'guarded' the 'Carrington Arms' at Ashby Folville, south of Melton Mowbray, Leicestershire, in the mid-1960s. This

was a replica of a V-1 'doodlebug'. The pub fell into disrepair for some time and the V-1 disappeared.

Most memorable of the few pubs that have had aircraft gracing their grounds was 'The Spitfire' at Upper Hill, near Leominster, Hereford. Landlord Percy Sheppard had long wanted a Spitfire and in 1967 his opportunity came. Mk XVI TD135 had been with 346 Squadron of the Air Training Corps at Tynemouth, and was in decaying state. It was salvaged and moved to the dump at RAF Dishforth, on the A1 near Ripon and here got into still worse state. It carried the codes 'NG-U' of 604 (County of Middlesex) Squadron and the legend 'One of The Few' underneath the cockpit. The hulk was offered for tender and Percy snapped it up for £25.

The replica V-1 'doodlebug' that was displayed outside the 'Carrington Arms' at Ashby Folville, near Melton Mowbray, in the 1960s. Ken Ellis collection

Spitfire XVI TD135 during its days with 346 Squadron Air Training Corps at Tynemouth. The 'NG' code is a legacy of its last operational unit, 604 (County of Middlesex) Squadron, Royal Auxiliary Air Force. MAP

From Tynemouth, TD135's fortunes turned downhill. By 1966 it was on the dump at RAF Dishforth, robbed of vital items. Ken Ellis collection

Above: *At Upper Hill Percy and friends worked hard on TD135 and with their limited resources brought the hulk back to life. The teardrop canopy always eluded them and a fairly crude, framed, mock-up was eventually settled on.* MAP

Below: *After the Spitfire, the Supermarine theme was continued with the acquisition of Swift F.4 WK275. This is still displayed at the Sheppard family's crane hire business in Upper Hill.* Ken Ellis

The Spitfire was moved to the pub, and he 'Red Lion' became 'The Spitfire' in onour of its new arrival. The aircraft eeded much work and Percy and friends et to, producing a very reasonable-look-ng static restoration. The bubble canopy lways defeated them and a somewhat gly, much-framed, version was put in lace. On hearing of the availability of upermarine Swift F.4 WK275 at Hatfield, erts, this too was acquired and moved to pper Hill, going alongside the Spitfire. adly, Percy died in 1975 and enthusi-sm for the aeroplanes waned, the two eing put up for auction. The Spitfire was old in the USA and is today to be found at eneseo in New York state under long rm restoration to flying condition. The wift stayed on with the family business nd still 'guards the gate' of what is today heppard's Crane Hire at Upper Hill.

A jet that may yet aspire to display : a drinking emporium is Lightning F.6 5928, currently held in storage at British erospace's airfield at Warton, Lancs. ere is the 'Lightning Club', a social club r the workforce and it is hoped that the eek machine will be put on display in the rounds of the club in due course.

Nightclubs have long had a need for teresting, odd or exciting attractions and recent years aircraft appear to have een added to the list of desirable 'deco-tions'. At 'Planet Holywood' just off eicester Square in London, among the tefacts of the stars can be found a real film star. 'Flying' here is a replica of *Little Nellie*, the famous Wallis WA-116 Agile autogyro used in the James Bond film *You Only Live Twice*. The original *Nellie*, G-ARZB, is treasured by Wing Comman-der Ken Wallis at his home in Norfolk, but this machine was assembled from spare components. Wallis (see also under Nor-wich Airport, above) flew *Nellie* in the sequences flown in Japan and at Elstree, doubling for '007' Sean Connery.

At Stamford, Lincolnshire, inside the newly-refurbished and renamed 'Hangar' can be found Robinson R-22 G-KENN while not far away at 'The Works' in Corby, Northants, Rockwell Commander 112A G-TCSL 'flies' over the dancing throngs and is placarded as a 'Rockwell WW2 Fighter'! Of smaller proportions is homebuilt Bede BD-5 Micro G-BDTT which is displayed in a similar fashion at 'Martini's' in Barrow-in-Furness, Cum-bria. A nightclub in Rayner's Lane, Lon-don, held a 'Cessna' of sorts and may well have displayed at least a 'homebuilt' heli-copter. Further investigation has been postponed as the 'entertainment' on offer includes 'Page Three Girls – Wet n' Wild' and divorces could be in the offing even if the research was for the noble cause of aviation!

An interesting note worth following up is the sale of Vickers Viscount Series 813 G-AZNA from Southend, Essex, for use in a nightclub in 1993 – did it achieve star-dom?

Above: *The real Wallis WA-116 Agile* Little Nellie *has been a popular performer at air displays. A 'replica' version 'flies' amid the glitz in London's 'Planet Hollywood'.* Ken Ellis Below: *Robinson R-22 G-KENN provides an interesting spectacle within 'The Hangar' night-club in Stamford, Lincolnshire.* The Hangar

THE SHEPLEY SPITFIRE

Not quite a 'plane and pint' as defined in the previous pages, but the pub 'The Shepley Spitfire' at Totley, south of Sheffield, is most unusual in that it is named after a presentation Spitfire and more importantly remembers a valiant local family. Jack Shepley and his wife lived in Woodthorpe Hall at Holmestead, immediately to the south of Totley. Like many, many families, their offspring were to quickly involve themselves in the war. Susan lost her life on the SS *Yorkshire*, when it was torpedoed – she chose to attend to injured and took her chances.

Flight Lieutenant George Rex Shepley is reported to have lost his life while single-handedly attacking "a large formation of enemy aircraft over Dunkirk". (The authors have been unable to put more details to this. Some losses during the Fall of France, late May to early June 1940, are incomplete due to lack of paperwork, but only a small number. Added to this is a confusing reference in one source, quoting that G R Shepley served with Bomber Command.)

On 8th and again on 11th August 1940 while flying Supermarine Spitfires with 152 Squadron from Warmwell, Dorset, Pilot Officer Douglas Clayton Shepley claimed a Messerschmitt Bf 109 in combat. His luck ran out on the 12th when he was seen to attack Junkers Ju 88s south of the Isle of Wight in Spitfire I K9999. He

was reported missing and is thought to have come down off St Katherine's Point. Douglas was the youngest of the Shepley offspring, and the third to lay down his life in a very short space of time.

As can be imagined, the losses hit the Shepley family and the local community hard. It was agreed that a most appropriate way to mark their sacrifice would be to raise money under the Ministry of Aircraft Production (MAP) 'Spitfire Fund' scheme. The target was £5,700 to 'buy' a Spitfire for the nation – a not inconsiderable sum in its day. The Shepley family donated heavily and in the local community their were cake sales, whist drives and many other events. It took just 15 weeks to raise the required sum.

Part of an order for 450 Mk I Spitfires placed on 22nd February 1940, W3649 was completed as a Mk VB and made its first flight on 1st August 1941. Painted with the word 'Shepley' in script underneath the cockpit, the Spitfire was issued to 6 Maintenance Unit at Brize Norton, Oxfordshire, on 5th August, for preparation for operations.

Its first use came from 16th August 1941 when it was issued to 602 (City of Glasgow) Squadron, Royal Auxiliary Air Force, then stationed at Kenley, Surrey. The unit was then under the command of Squadron Leader A C 'Al' Deere DFC*. W3649 would have carried 'LO-' squadron code letters.

Fighters moved swiftly between units

particularly during the early years of the war, meeting attrition and tactical needs. W3649 moved on to 303 (Polish) Squadron on 28th October 1941, based at Northolt, Middlesex and flying with 'RF-' codes. The stay with 303 was brief, 'Shepley' returned to Kenley on 24th November, this time to be flown by personnel from 485 Squadron, Royal New Zealand Air Force, with the codes 'OU-'. Commanding the unit at this time was Squadron Leader E P Wells, DFC, RA.

During the mid-afternoon of 28th March 1942, 'Shepley' was allocated to Group Captain F V Beamish DSO, DFC, AFC as part of a fighter patrol in force. It was to be the last sortie for both pilot and machine as the entry in 485's Operations Record Book (ORB) attests:

Operations Record Book

485 (NZ) Squadron

Squadron, led by Group/Capt Beamish DSO, DFC, AFC, and with the rest of Wing took off at 17.00 hrs on Fighter Patrol Cap Gris-Nez and Gravelines. Landfall just S of Gris-Nez was made at 17.30 hrs. Some forty to fifty E/A were seen. There were chiefly FW.190.s with some ME.109.s at heights varying from 15,000 to 20,000 ft in loose formations of pairs and fours, and were just about to dive on some of our outgoing fighters (Biggin Hill Wing). G/Capt. Beamish turned the Wing sharply to port to intercept these Huns, and W/Cdr Boyd and his No.2, who were on the outside of the turn, attacked two FW.190.s and became separated from the Wing. Individual combat immediately ensued. G/Capt. Beamish, who was Red 1, followed by F/L. Grant, DFM, and F/Sgt Liken, both of 485 Squadron dived to attack two FW.190.s from 19,000 ft These dived away and were lost. The Group Capt. then orbited inland 5 miles off Calais at 13,000 ft, Red 3 and 4 were lost. When a FW.190 came in to attack the Group Capt., F/Sgt. Liken warned the G/Capt. over the phone. F/L. Grant whose R/T did not function from take-off then opened up, and pulling his nose up gave the FW.190 a two second burst in the belly from about 50 yards range just as the Hun opened fire on the G/Capt. Strikes were seen in the port wing and under the fuselage of the FW.190 and it dived away vertically, pouring greyish blue smoke from its engine, and a large piece which seemed to be the left aileron blew off, and the cannon hole in the port wing appeared to be widening as it went down. F/L. Grant observed the Spitfire of the G/Capt. to be hit in the underpart of the fuselage and its nose was slightly down. It was proceeding out over the coast about 5 miles ENE of Calais, heading approximately N. West. F/L. Grant weaved in a figure of eight behind and above, covering it. The G/Capt.'s aircraft was now trailing a little smoke at 13,000 ft, and another FW.190 came in to attack but F/L. Grant attacked it with cannon from 150 yds. range from port quarter astern, and the FW.190 shuddered, continued on its course for a brief period and suddenly blew up. The G/Capt. was heard by S/L. Finucane asking for a fix and someone advised his to steer 310 but Kenley Ops. did not receive this call. G/Capt. Beamish failed to return.

And so the Shepley Spitfire came to an end. The Shepley family and the locals of Totley and Holmestead would be unaware of this as after the presentation of a photograph of 'their' aircraft, like other Spitfire Funds, those involved were not privy to the operational history of the aircraft. While many might have hoped that it would have a long and valiant operational life, most probably knew in their heart of hearts that if fighter pilots faced severe odds, so did their mounts.

In the late 1970s, Totley was aware that it was to get a brand new pub and before too long the idea of calling it the 'The Shepley Spitfire' gelled and preparations were made accordingly. It was opened in 1979 by Seymour Shepley, the surviving son of Jack.

Within the pub can be found a wide range of Spitfire paintings and models. In

A modern pub with a 1940s background, 'The Shepley Spitfire'. Ken Ellis

the entrance lobby can be found a picture of Spitfire VB W3649 'Shepley', a copy of the photograph that MAP would have supplied along with a certificate to mark the hand over of the fund. Also here is a framed collection of 1941 press cuttings relating to the Shepley family and the fund raising to achieve the Spitfire. Within the main bar is an outline history of W3649 and a copy of the 485 Squadron ORB for 28th March 1942.

Outside, the pub sign includes a fair rendition of a Mk V Spitfire, carrying the serial W3649. The codes carried are 'F-VB' which is assumed to be based upon the aircraft's designation – an F (Mk) VB. ('VB-' was used by 14 Operational Training Unit, a Wellington bomber unit.)

While it is a modern pub, 'The Shepley Spitfire' pays honest tribute to great sacrifice and the endeavours of a community. Its landlord and staff are knowledgeable of the events the pub name commemorates and are always happy to pass on details to those who visit, to sup, eat and ponder.

'The Shepley Spitfire' pub sign shows W3649, although the codes are fictitious. Ken Ellis

YOU WANT MORE?

Hints and help on
how to continue the
arduous research...

YOU WANT MORE?

A warning for the unwary; pub names present many misleading traps. Here are just a few examples: 'The Blenheim' at Epsom commemorates the 1930 Derby winner, 'The Highflyer' at Ely another race horse, 'The Comet' at Shrewsbury is named after a stagecoach which once served that city, the 'Glocester (sic) Flying Machine' is another stagecoach reference, and 'The Viscount' near the Vauxhall factory at Ellesmere Port, Cheshire was inspired by a 1960s car design.

Conversely, a few pubs are aviation-related although their names do not reveal the fact. One such is 'The Berinsfield Arms' in Oxfordshire. Its Spitfire and Lockheed P-38 Lightning sign remembers nearby RAF Mount Farm. The sign of 'The Bell' at Halton Holegate, Lincolnshire shows a Lancaster over the pub on approach to RAF Spilsby and the dedication '207 and 44 Squadrons'. 'Fagans', in Sheffield is named after Joe Fagan, an ex-Halifax pilot and former landlord.

One of the pre-requisites for research into aeronautical pubs and inns is *Yellow Pages*. Large libraries will have the entire collection – more than 60 volumes these days – if you feel so inspired. They will help with the seemingly obviously-related pubs – but bear in mind the above warnings and many other examples in the main text. *Yellow Pages* will, not of course, help with tracking down former 'Watering holes'! (See under that chapter for some hints and warnings about following them up.) Another very useful tome to have around is BT's *The Phone Book Companion* which helps to track down dialling codes.

Also invaluable – and of great use in the research undertaken for this book – are the many Tourist Information Centres up and down the country. Directory enquiries will find a suitable one close to your needs and most of them have good details of pubs in their area.

A good book to have for reference to pub names in general is the excellent *Pub Names of Britain* by Leslie Dunkling and Gordon Wright (Orion, London 1994). First published as *A Dictionary of Pub Names* in 1987 this gives brief details of the origins of over 10,000 hostelries. Of a very different nature, but also very well worth getting hold of is *Inn of The Few*, Katherine Preston, Spellmount, 1993, giving the story of 'The White Hart' at Brasted, near Biggin Hill.

For information on pubs and much more, then membership of the Campaign for Real Ale (CAMRA) should be considered. There are branches all over the country and CAMRA produces a good range of books. (Contact them at 34 Alma Road, St Albans, Herts, AL1 3BW.) Chief among their book range is the annual *Good Beer Guide* which is a mine of information and widely available from bookshops.

GAZETTEER

A guide to
aeronautical pubs
past and present

GAZETTEER

Herewith a listing of the aeronautical pubs and inns mentioned within the main text and also others that, by their name, *seem* to have an obvious aviation connection. As explained in the introduction and in 'You Want More?', further research is essential into this subject and inputs from readers will be greatly appreciated.

This section serves as a guide to the pubs that are *believed* to be current (marked with a ❏) or no longer extant, or renamed (marked with a ■). Addresses and telephone numbers are given for those believed to be current, but a 'phone call ahead is *always advised* to save disappointment. There seems to be a growing trend for pubs and inns to go into telephone directories not by the name of the hostelry, but under the publican's name – this does not help when checking up! For ease of reference 'The' has been omitted from those pubs and inns starting that way. Finally, pubs mentioned in the main text are given a page reference.

'The Britannia' at Patchway, not far from where the airliner was built. This is a good example of a name 'hinting' at an aviation connection. In reality most of the 'Britannias' in Britain are named after the lady who appears on the back of coins.
Rod Priddle

BY NAME

Top: *Cause and effect. 'The Air Balloon Tavern' in Bristol is located in Air Balloon Road. To what event does the road owe its name?* Rod Priddle

Above: *'The Aviator' at St Ives, Cambridgeshire.* Bill Taylor

Top: 'The Comet Hotel' at Hatfield, Hertfordshire, just south of the famous former airfield. Within can be found many items to remind visitors of the de Havilland products that were built there. Ken Ellis

Below: In the car park of 'The Comet' is a superb model of the DH.88 Comet racer G-ACSS Grosvenor House (see page 25). The real thing is kept by the Shuttleworth Collection at Old Warden, Bedfordshire, in taxiable condition. Jerome Knight

Above: 'The Harrier' at Gunthorpe, near Peterborough, is underneath the approach to RAF Wittering, home of the RAF's UK-based Harrier force. Bill Taylor

Below: A view of the rear fuselage of the impressive B-17 Flying Fortress scale replica that adorns the top of the bar in Leicester's 'Meridian'. Ken Ellis

Above: *Lutterworth's 'Red Arrow', close to the former Bitteswell airfield.* Dave Smith
Below: *The 'Red Lion Inn' at East Kirkby, famed 'watering hole'.* Mike Ingham

Left, top: *Within the 'White Swan' at Harringworth, Northants, is a detailed display devoted to the men and machines of the 315th Troop Carrier Wing, compiled by local historians. The 315th were based 'up the hill' at Spanhoe Lodge.*

Left, bottom: *The inside of 'The Shepley Spitfire' includes many items of Spitfire memorabilia, including prints and paintings, models and press cuttings.* Both Ken Ellis

Above, left: *A section of the 'Gibson Room' within the 'Lion and Royal' at Navenby, Lincolnshire. Guy Gibson was billeted in the pub during his time at nearby RAF Digby.* Mike Ingham

Above, right: *Part of the extensive displays illustrating the airfield at Deenethorpe and the 401st Bombardment Group to be found within the 'Wheatsheaf' at Upper Benefield, Northamptonshire.* Ken Ellis

Above: 'The Reindeer' at Long Benington, a Bottesford 'watering hole'. Below: 'The Sunderland Flying Boat' at Sunderland, Tyne & Wear. Both Ken Ellis

BY COUNTY

Pubs are listed by present day administrative county boundaries.

England

Bedfordshire:	'Airman', 'Balloon', 'Glider', 'Parachute', 'Tiger Moth', 'Windsock'
Berkshire:	'Lands End', 'Merlin'
Cambridgeshire:	'Aviator', 'Bird', 'Chequers', 'Eagle', 'Harrier' (x 2), 'Pear Tree'
Cleveland:	'Astronaut', 'Spitfire', 'Telstar'
Cornwall:	'Ops Room', 'Swordfish'
Cumbria:	'Martini's'
Derbyshire:	'Ladybower', 'Merlin'
Devon:	'Ark Royal', 'Walrus'
Dorset:	'Fighter Pilot', 'Flying Boat', 'St Leonard's Hotel'
Durham:	'Hope'
Essex:	'B-52 Bar', 'King's Head', 'Red Beret'
Gloucestershire:	'Air Balloon', 'Air Balloon Tavern', 'Airport Tavern', 'Bristol Bulldog', 'Britannia', 'Concorde', 'Double-O-Two', 'Flying Machine', 'Happy Landings', 'Jet and Whittle', 'Lamb Inn', 'Pegasus', 'Red Baron', 'Wayfarer'
Hampshire:	'Chopper Arms', 'Cody's Tree', 'Dakotas', 'Flying Boat', 'Harrier', 'Invincible', 'Owl and Crescent', 'Swordfish', 'Wyvern'
Hereford & Worcester:	'Red Lion', 'Spitfire', 'Star Hotel'
Hertfordshire:	'Comet', 'Jet', 'Woodman'
Isle of Wight:	'Propeller Inn'
Kent:	'Battle of Britain' (x 3), 'Canopus', 'Cat and Custard Pot', 'Flying Saucer', 'Startled Saint', 'Tiger Moth', 'White Hart'
Leicestershire:	'Airmans Rest', 'Balloon', 'Flying Lancaster', 'Flying Saucer', 'Meridian', 'Red Arrow', 'Sir Frank Whittle'
Lincolnshire:	'Bell', 'Black Horse', 'George Hotel', 'Hangar', 'Jug and Bottle', 'Lion and Royal', 'Petwood House Hotel', 'Saracen's Head', 'Turner Arms Hotel', 'White Hart' (x 2), 'Wild Life'
London (Greater):	'Aerodrome', 'Air Hostess', 'Airman', 'Britannia', 'Catch 22',

	'Chopper', 'Escape', 'Fairey Firefly', 'Flying Eagle', 'Flying Machine', 'Happy Landings', 'Hind and Hart', 'Jumbo Jet', 'Leefe Robinson', 'Planet Hollywood', 'Propeller', 'Silver Bullet'
Manchester (Greater):	'Airport' (x2), 'Heald Green', 'Tiger Moth', 'Vulcan'
Midlands, West:	'Battle of Britain', 'Pilot'
Merseyside:	'Caernarvon Castle', 'Flying Saucer'
Norfolk:	'Ambassador Hotel', 'Blue Lion', 'Eagle', 'Eagle Hotel', 'Ferry Inn', 'Gallon Pot', 'Hero', 'Ship'
Northamptonshire:	'Aviator Hotel', 'Exeter Arms', 'Wheatsheaf', 'White Swan', 'Works'
Nottinghamshire:	'Air Hostess', 'Concorde', 'Early Bird', 'Flying Bedstead', 'Gondola', 'Harrier', 'Reindeer'
Oxfordshire:	'Air Balloon', 'Berinsfield Arms'
Suffolk:	'Buck', 'Five Bells', 'Flying Boat', 'Flying Fortress', 'Fox', 'Sir Douglas Bader', 'Swan', 'Triple Plea', 'Warwick'
Surrey:	'Cunningham', 'Flight Tavern', 'Gatwick'
Sussex (East):	'Gatwick Hilton', 'Wellington'
Sussex (West):	'Bader Arms', 'Dolphin', 'Green Dragon', 'Guinea Pig', 'Old Ship', 'Victoria Hotel'
Tyne & Wear:	'Balloon', 'Sunderland Flying Boat'
Warwickshire:	'Baginton Oak', 'Jet and Whittle'
Wiltshire:	'Flying Monk', 'Harrier'
Yorkshire (East):	'Barnes Wallis', 'Buccaneer', 'Ye Olde Red Lion Hotel'
Yorkshire (North):	'Betty's Bar', 'Blacksmith's Arms', 'Bombers', 'Busby Stoop Inn', 'Cayley Arms', 'Flying Legends', 'Memphis Belle'
Yorkshire (South):	'Fagans', 'Flarepath', 'Pathfinder', 'Shepley Spitfire'
Yorkshire (West):	'Pathfinder Hotel'

Scotland

Fife:	'Tipsy Nipper'
Grampian:	'Runway'
Strathclyde:	'Viscount'

Wales

Dyfed:	'Flying Boat'
Glamorgan (Mid):	'Vulcan Inn'
Glamorgan (South):	'Old Airport'
Gwynedd:	'Dakota Restaurant'
Powys,	'Gremlin Hotel'

WHAT'S IN A BREW?

Another theme that needs more sleuthing. CAMRA's *Good Beer Guide* (see page 72) has a beers index in which brews are listed by name. Independent brewer Shepherd Neame of Faversham currently brew 'Spitfire Ale' and used to produce 'Dam Buster'. There must have been many more 'specials' brewed – perhaps only for a short while – by other brewers up and down the land. Another exercise for readers to get their tongues into for the second edition!

We hope you have enjoyed this Midland Publishing book. Our titles are carefully edited and designed for you by knowledgeable and enthusiastic specialists, with over 20 years of experience. Further titles are in the course of preparation but we would welcome ideas on what you would like to see. If you have a manuscript or project that requires publishing, we should be happy to consider it; brief details initially please.

In addition, our associate company, Midland Counties Publications, offers an exceptionally wide range of aviation, astronomy, military and railway books/videos for sale by mail-order around the world. For a copy of the appropriate catalogue, please write, telephone or fax to:
Midland Counties Publications
Unit 3 Maizefield, Hinckley Fields, Hinckley, Leics, LE10 1YF
Tel: 01455 233 747; Fax: 01455 841 805

WRECKS & RELICS
15th Edition

Ken Ellis

Wrecks & Relics has been a cherished part of the world of aviation heritage since the first edition was published 35 years ago. The 15th edition, expanded and refined, will be much sought after by enthusiasts in the UK and Ireland.

The book lists and traces the movements of thousands of aircraft held in museums, preserved with individuals, in use as gate guardians, instructional airframes, on fire dumps etc, in the United Kingdom and Ireland, and on RAF bases overseas.

Includes museums with opening times, BAPC member groups, BAPC/ IAHC registers, and enormously useful indexes by both aircraft type and location. New for this edition is an examination of export aircraft, still further improved layout for even easier reference and an expanded photographs section.

Previous editions still in print:
12th edition (1990) 252pp
£9.95
14th edition (1994) 336pp   **£12.95**

Laminated Hardback
210 x 148 mm, 350 pages
with about 200 photos.
1 85780 047 8   May
£14.95

BRITISH AIRFIELD BUILDINGS OF WWII

Aviation Pocket Guide 1

Graham Buchan Innes

The world of airfield buildings is one of constant fascination to enthusiasts. Until now, references on this subject have been the domain of very specialist works, or to be partially found within high price books. All of this has conspired to put off a whole army of people who have a thirst for such knowledge.

British Airfield Buildings is the answer to this need and in a genuinely pocket-size form. From control towers, to hangars, to defensive strongpoints, barrack blocks, maintenance buildings to the humble latrine, it provides an illustration of a *surviving* example, highlighting details and other styles of similar building.

Over 200 illustrations with brief but informative captions take the reader for an excursion through a typical wartime station.

British Airfield Buildings provides an ideal primer to a subject close to the heart of all enthusiasts.

Softback
148 x 105 mm, 128 pages
230 b/w photographs
1 85780 026 5   Available
£5.95

AVIATION MUSEUMS OF BRITAIN
Aviation Pocket Guide 2

Ken Ellis

All aviation enthusiasts look forward to visiting an aviation museum and often plan their journeys to make sure that one (or more!) can be taken in. *Aviation Museums of Britain* provides the important information that most people need to know before setting out: When is it open? Which ones are open off-season? Is there a cafe? Is there somewhere for the kids to play? Is there a shop to browse around? This book answers all of these questions and of course provides an easy-to-read review of what aircraft exhibits are on show and a breakdown of other displays, features and themes within Britain's 80 aviation museums.

The book goes much further in helping the reader plan a full day – or weekend – away with suggestions of other attractions nearby, allowing *all* of the family to find something of interest.

An invaluable guide, opening up many ideas and possibilities.
A constant companion in the glove box or the pocket.

Softback
148 x 105mm, 128 pages
112 b/w photographs
1 85780 038 X   Available
£5.95

DISCOVER AVIATION TRAILS

Aviation Pocket Guide 4

Paul Shaw

Interest in aviation museums, airfields used and disused, memorials and other aeronautical venues has never been higher. Enthusiasts are keen to know what to look for and how. Until now, their plans to tour the country relied very much on their own researches – with the risk of missing many 'gems'.

Now an answer is to hand in the popular Aviation Pocket Guide format, a pocket sized collection of twelve regional tours that can be undertaken by car in a day, or over a weekend with 'add ons'. The suggested tours span the country, offering enthusiasts a 'local' to investigate and a many possibilities to be taken up on holiday: Cornwall; Derbyshire/Leicestershire/Notts; Essex; Lincoln; Lincolnshire; London; Manchester and Cheshire; Norfolk; Northamptonshire; Southern Scotland; South Wales; Yorkshire.

With each tour come plenty of suggestions, each carefully put together to allow for a 'gentle' pace. An ideal travelling companion for enthusiasts of all ages.

Softback
148 x 105 mm, 128 pages
b/w and colour photos
1 85780 049 4   May
£6.95

FlyPast

Britain's top-selling aviation monthly has a very special place in the hearts of enthusiasts all over the world.

Through the years, readers have come to regard *FlyPast* as the magazine covering the world of aviation history, especially its coverage of *living* history. *FlyPast* has never contented itself with just monitoring news of aircraft and events worldwide as they happen, its editorial staff and a network of renowned contributors have built up a reputation as news and opinion makers in their own right. All of this combines to make *FlyPast* the journal that *leads* in the fascinating world of aviation history, museums, displays, operators and aircraft. Don't stand on the touchlines, *take part* with *FlyPast*!

..FlyPast the journal that leads in the fascinating world of aviation history...

Monthly

Free Membership

In addition, as a subscriber you'll become an automatic member of the *FlyPast* club. This exclusive club was launched to offer its members fantastic benefits. There's a regular newsletter, special privileges, club discounts on selected items, museum visits, lectures and much, much more.

To ensure you never miss an issue of *FlyPast* place a regular order with your newsagent or take out a post-free postal subscription. See the current issue of *FlyPast* for rates or contact:- Subscription Dept., Key Publishing Ltd., PO Box 100, Stamford, Lincs., PE9 1XQ. Tel:- 01780 55131, Fax:- 01780 57261 or EMail:- subs@keymags.demon.co.uk.

Full of Facts, Full of Memories